Massacring Indians

Massacring Indians

From Horseshoe Bend
to Wounded Knee

ROGER L. NICHOLS

University of Oklahoma Press : Norman

On the front, top: "Gathering up the dead of the battlefield of Wounded Knee, S.D." (detail). Northwestern Photographic Co., January 3, 1891(?). X-31464. *Bottom:* "Sitting Bull's Camp" (detail). D. F. [David Francis] Barry, 1880s. B-242. Both images courtesy The Denver Public Library, Western History Collection.

Library of Congress Cataloging-in-Publication Data

Names: Nichols, Roger L., author.
Title: Massacring Indians : from Horseshoe Bend to Wounded Knee / Roger L. Nichols.
Description: Norman : University of Oklahoma Press, [2021] | Includes bibliographical references and index. | Summary: "Examines the unique circumstances and common elements of ten significant massacres committed by U.S. Army units against American Indians, and presents them as part of a larger pattern of U.S. military aggression"—Provided by publisher.
Identifiers: LCCN 2020038659 | ISBN 978-0-8061-6864-7 (paperback)
Subjects: LCSH: United States. Army—History—19th century. | Massacres—United States—History—19th century. | Indians of North America—Violence against—United States—History—19th century. | Indians of North America—Wars—United States—History—19th century.
Classification: LCC E81 .N525 2021 | DDC 970.004/97—dc23
LC record available at https://lccn.loc.gov/2020038659

To
Mackenzie, Maverick, and Olivia Hawk,
Jackson, Raelynn Rhoten, and Brooks Bernth
and to Marilyn, the world's best editor,
critic, and partner

Contents

Acknowledgments

Publishing a book is a long process, and along the way many people have helped. Librarians, archivists, and staff from several organizations have graciously helped me locate material and photographs. These include the State Historical Society of Wisconsin, History Nebraska of that state, the Abraham Lincoln Presidential Library in Illinois, the University of Arizona Library, the Library of Congress, and the Smithsonian Institution. Members of the University of Oklahoma staff always make book publishing as pleasant and worry free as possible. Special thanks are due to Alessandra Jacobi Tamulevich, acquisitions editor for American Indian and Latin American studies; Steven B. Baker, who oversaw the publication process; Kathy Burford Lewis, who copyedited the manuscript with skill and grace; and cartographer Tom Jonas, who provided the map locating each of the incidents discussed in the text. Last, but never least, thanks to my wife, Marilyn, who read these pages more often than anyone should have to and helped prevent any tangled prose or muddled logic.

Tucson, Arizona
May 2020

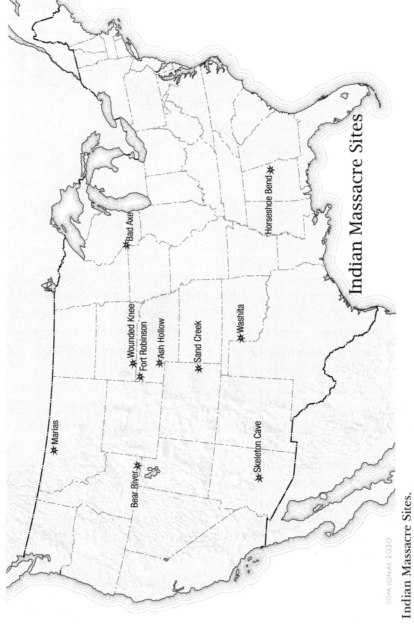

Indian Massacre Sites.
Cartography by Tom Jonas.

Introduction

During much of U.S. history most Americans would have been surprised to see massacres of Indians included as part of the nation's story. In fact, many tend to reorder the words "massacre" and "Indian" into "Indian massacre." "Massacre" has several overlapping meanings. One dictionary defines it as "an instance of killing a number of usually helpless or unresisting human beings under circumstances of atrocity or cruelty." Another calls it "the killing of human beings by indiscriminate slaughter, murder of numbers with cruelty or atrocity."[1] More pejorative than neutral, and frequently used as propaganda, the word has become a kind of simplistic shorthand label for complex situations and is often thrown around carelessly. In this study I use "massacre" to describe battles in which U.S. military forces killed large numbers of Indian women and children during the fighting, killed unarmed Indian men trying to surrender or escape from the battle, committed atrocities during or after the combat, and confiscated or destroyed the villagers' food and property. Although historians have used the term sparingly, the pioneers used it repeatedly to describe Indian triumphs in contrast to white military successes, which they called victories.

For readers who might be offended by references to American military actions as massacres, the vicious destruction of an entire Indian village in California should be convincing evidence that this charge is not just political correctness run amok. In late March 1846 a heavily armed army exploring party led by Captain John C. Frémont camped at Peter Lassen's ranch in northern California. While there, the captain heard reports that nearly a thousand Indians had gathered just a few miles away and were preparing to attack the local settlers. In fact, a Wintus Indian camp with about five hundred people stood on the bank of the Sacramento River not far from the ranch. There the Indians held religious ceremonies that they hoped would improve their annual salmon catch, not war dances to prepare for a raid, as fearful whites had reported. Without investigating the situation, on the morning of April 15, 1846, Frémont led his seventy-four well-armed soldiers, Indian guides, and five local volunteers in an unprovoked attack on the Wintus camp.

When village leaders saw Frémont's force approaching, the men formed a line as they tried to protect their families. As the attack began, the captain gave the order "to ask no quarter and to give none." The troops began firing their long-range rifles while staying well beyond the reach of the Indians' arrows. After the first murderous volley, the soldiers charged into the village, using their sabers and other sidearms to begin killing at close range. One of the attackers remembered that "the [five civilian] volunteers . . . then commenced a scene of slaughter which was unequalled in the West. The bucks, squaws, and papooses were shot down like sheep." Another expedition member wrote that when some of the Indians fled, "Kit Carson and the Delaware Indians," who were mounted, "literally tomahawked their way through the flying Indians." Meanwhile, the rest of Frémont's men "kept up a continual fire on the Indians who had jumped into the river and were swimming across. It was a slaughter." Carson remembered the incident as "a perfect butchery."[2]

Although they tried to blame the slaughter on the Delaware scouts and the five civilians with the troops, the soldiers' rifle fire and saber charge killed the most people. When the shooting ended, the attackers had suffered no casualties, which suggests that the Indians were so poorly armed that they could not have been preparing to raid the settlers. Instead they had camped along the river for their yearly fish harvest. Certainly "massacre" is the only honest term to describe Frémont's action.

The best way to understand the Indian massacres committed by American military units during the nineteenth century recounted in this book is to see them as part of a process that historians call "settler colonialism" and the government actions associated with it. Patrick Wolfe, a leading proponent of that theory, described how federal officials acted consciously to speed territorial expansion and take land from the indigenous people. Even before writing the Constitution, American political leaders established two systems for doing that. The 1785 Land Ordinance promoted land purchases, while the Northwest Ordinance of 1787 provided government for newly settled areas. Both these measures responded to the demands of a growing settler population of pioneer farmers. The ongoing process of invasion and territorial expansion persuaded officials that they needed to take the Indians' land as well as to erase their distinctive cultural practices and identity. That eventually resulted in moving the tribal people onto isolated reservations and into a subservient position in American society.[3] The notion of settler colonialism accurately and effectively depicts the acquiring of tribal lands and undermining of tribal existence. It also explains how and why indigenous people came to fight wars of resistance in the face of U.S. determination to push them aside.

Scholars have characterized those conflicts in several ways. Some view the federal system for dealing with the Indians as poorly planned, disorganized, incompetent, and corrupt. Others point out that the nineteenth-century assimilation policy, while culturally destructive and poorly administered, was meant to preserve Indians, not exterminate them. They admit that particular incidents such as the battles at Bad Axe, Ash Hollow, and Sand Creek were massacres but claim that those represent outliers rather than examples of routine military practices in regard to the Indians.[4] Gary Anderson offered the modern term "ethnic cleansing" as what he considered a more nuanced way to look at the issue. That term accurately describes Indian removal or murders by the Texas Rangers.[5]

Activist Indian writers have strenuously argued that American actions toward the Indians represented genocide. They quote Thomas Jefferson's bellicose 1807 warning to Indians living near Detroit: if the United States had to go to war against any tribe, it would not stop fighting until "that tribe is exterminated, or driven beyond the Mississippi." He threatened that if the Indians went to war with the United States "they will kill some of us [but] we shall destroy all of them."[6] Those involved in genocide studies have argued repeatedly over definitions of intent, means, and results of national policies and actions, yet they agree that U.S. Indian policy was a clear premodern example of that practice.[7] Jeffrey Ostler recently wrote that the government came to believe that "genocidal war . . . was necessary" because of Indian resistance.[8]

While agreeing that the government's tactics in dealing with the Indians were destructive, anthropologist James Clifton boldly rejected those charges. In 1989 he wrote that "in the over 200 years it has existed as a nation, no U.S. administration from George Washington to Ronald Reagan has ever approved, tolerated or abetted a policy aimed at the deliberate, systematic extermination of Indians."[9] At first glance this appears true, but it overlooks the fact that federal actions or inactions brought land loss as well as physical and cultural destruction to tens of thousands of indigenous people throughout American history even without any policies or programs designed to do that.

This study agrees with Clifton. Although incidents of genocidal violence occurred, rather than seeking to destroy Indians, the United States has always suffered from a kind of national schizophrenia when dealing with them. Despite the frustrated outbursts of some frontier commanders, and pioneer citizens' demands for exterminating the Indians, neither the federal government nor much of American society ever supported that policy. Instead many people accepted the idea that Indians belonged to an inferior and dying race and that they would eventually disappear despite efforts to help them. This meant that the nation had a moral obligation to ease their passage. A smaller number of people hoped that, given enough time and help, the Indians might become "civilized" and enter the general society. Usually the federal government preferred negotiations for land to war, because military action was just too expensive. Searching for ways to deal with the Indians, Congress spent tens of millions of dollars on programs designed to persuade tribal people to change their cultures and economies and copy their white neighbors, who then moved into their homelands. Because the legislators never bothered to ask the Indians about their willingness to accept those programs, they usually failed.

The effort to acculturate the Indians failed for several reasons. First, the indigenous people wanted to remain independent and rejected white values and practices. Second, a large percent of the American public feared, hated, or loathed Indians as dangerous "savages," called for their extermination, and repeatedly launched vicious attacks on tribal people. Third, the national policy of territorial expansion conflicted directly with Indian landholdings and uses. In the face of Indian refusal to accept the federal programs, the demands of greedy and violent pioneers, and its own expansionist goals, the federal government never developed carefully reasoned policies, rarely implemented its programs effectively, and failed to restrain the citizens' hatred and violence toward the indigenous people. That led to repeated violence when Indians fought to defend themselves and their land from the white invaders. As U.S. troops campaigned to end the interracial violence, they committed the repeated massacres examined here.

American history before 1900 is a chronicle of territorial expansion, rapid population growth, and repeated, often relentless, warfare with the Indians. From the initial 1607 skirmishing between the Powhatan Indians and the English invaders at Jamestown through the last sorry spectacle of military action at Wounded Knee in 1890, the record is one of vicious interracial conflict between whites and Indians. The invasion and land grabs that resulted from settler colonialism against the Indians during the colonial era led to hundreds of minor raids and skirmishes between pioneers and Indians. That violence, in turn, created hatred and fear among both peoples. For the whites the Declaration of Independence highlighted early American attitudes when it referred to "the merciless Indian Savages whose known rule of warfare is an undistinguished destruction of all ages, sexes and conditions."[10]

Even as they tried to defend themselves from the invading pioneers, many Indian tribes lived in a state of repeated wars with each other. Most of the village societies lived in armed camps and honored skill in hunting and warfare. They had elaborate ceremonies for men preparing for battle, during which they painted themselves. After the fighting they participated in public rites of purification, celebration, and mourning. Young men who were not recognized as warriors were not considered good marriage partners in some communities until they had proven their bravery by killing an enemy. Strong cultural traditions demanding clan revenge and military retaliation for real or perceived wrongs encouraged raiding and violence against neighboring tribes and the encroaching pioneers, while the village chiefs had little authority to end such raiding. Historically, the Indians' record of intertribal conflict nearly matched the record of the colonists.[11]

Describing the situation in 1776, historian Jeffrey Ostler wrote that "America was born fighting Indians."[12] The legacy of colonial frontier warfare shaped the actions and policies of early national leaders. George Washington, Thomas Jefferson, and others recognized that the nation's mostly rural citizens wanted, even required, land and based their policies toward the tribal people on the need for continuing territorial expansion. From the start George Washington recommended a policy of "being on good terms with the Indians, and the propriety of purchasing their Lands in preference to attempting to drive them by force of arms out of their Country."[13]

That view faded quickly in 1790 when a series of raids on pioneers traveling down the Ohio River brought demands for protection from Indian attacks, setting the nation's agenda for relations with the tribes. When the government made few serious efforts to stop the pioneers' repeated invasions of tribal homelands, the villagers tried to drive the invaders away. Their raids led to retaliation by frontier militias or federal troops that began a cycle of interracial violence. Washington recognized this in 1796 when he lamented that nothing "short of a Chinese wall, or a line of troops, will restrain Land jobbers, and the encroachment of settlers upon the Indian Territory."[14]

By the 1780s, when the United States gained its independence, these two militaristic societies had experienced generations of conflict with each other, which bred fear and hatred on both sides. During the colonial era wars, Indians and their French allies raided New England settlements and took captives to Canada for ransom. Some of the survivors wrote lurid tales that described the indigenous peoples' indiscriminate slaughter of women and children and included supposed incidents of Indians torturing their prisoners. These stories fixed popular images of the Indians as dangerous and cruel savages. By the time of national independence, most Euro-Americans had accepted the idea that Indians tortured and massacred their victims in the frequent interracial battles, while whites gained well-deserved victories in combat. Thus Indian successes became massacres in the stories about nineteenth-century wars, events at Fort Dearborn (1812), Raisin River (1813), and Fort Mims (1813), and the deaths of people such as Francis Dade in 1836, John Grattan in 1854, William Fetterman in 1866, and George Armstrong Custer in 1876.

This nineteenth-century view of Indian victories as massacres ignored the reality that armed whites killed many more Native Americans than the reverse. In fact, in its report after completing the census of 1890, in which it declared that the frontier had ended, the U.S. Bureau of the Census reported that the United States had fought forty wars with Indians since independence.[15] That was about one conflict for every three years of America's first hundred years as a nation. Even more to the point, the army stated that between 1865 and 1890 it had been involved in about 1,000 engagements with indigenous groups. Other compilations include hundreds of battles and massacres.[16] The lists present indisputable evidence that American civilians killed as many Indians or more than did U.S. troops.

Despite all that, formal military actions get the most attention, appearing as the "Indian wars" in many histories. How these conflicts came to be called wars is unclear. Article I of the U.S. Constitution gives Congress the sole "Power to declare war," to "raise and support armies," and "to suppress Insurrection and repel Invasion."[17] Congress never declared war on any tribe during the nineteenth century despite repeatedly referring to the tribes as nations. Indians were not considered part of American society, so they could not have joined an insurrection against the government. Nor could they invade the United States, because they lived within it. In fact, just the opposite happened: the pioneers invaded tribal lands. Perhaps Congress refrained from declaring war because the Indians never took part in any insurrections or invasions. Whatever the reasons for congressional inaction, presidents from Washington on authorized military campaigns against many indigenous groups.

As a result, the U.S. Army and various militia units fought Indians from the 1790s until the end of the nineteenth century. This study examines ten of those conflicts, which constitute virtually all the major massacres of Indians committed by the army. It examines battles from Alabama west to Arizona and from Arizona north to Montana and Idaho. Each chapter places the event in its local context, analyzes a single massacre, and, where possible, makes comparisons with the other incidents, seeking to find patterns that may emerge beyond the mere violence and confusion of battle. Many of these events have received book-length attention, but almost always only as isolated incidents. This book presents them as parts of a larger pattern of aggression and the actions of a weak or uncaring national leadership unable or unwilling to deal effectively with the indigenous people.

The narrative presents the circumstances and motivations of the soldiers and militiamen or volunteers in federal service. It provides examples of troops who received inadequate training and inattentive or
incompetent oversight by their officers, who demonstrated an eagerness
to punish Indians, seeking personal glory, as they led careless attacks on
the wrong village or band to explain some of the killings of civilians. The
chapters compare and contrast incidents in which noncombatants died as
a result of specific orders or tactics, cases where the troops ignored
orders, and instances where they suffered accidentally because of prox-
imity to the actual combat. The analysis also includes the violent actions
of Indian allies and auxiliaries serving with the troops. It highlights
Americans' varied responses to news of these massacres at the time and
modern public memories of the events.

My thesis is that these conflicts must be called massacres because
they involved attacks on villages whose chiefs thought they were at
peace or included the slaughter of civilians or of fighting men trying to
escape or surrender, the commission of battlefield atrocities by the
troops, and their destruction of Indian food, clothing, lodges, and
other property. Those actions went far beyond accepted formal military
tactics for combat between soldiers and Indians. For example, volunteer
units composed of pioneers who hated the Indians committed murders
and atrocities at Sand Creek and Bear River. In some cases, the attacks
began as a planned military strike on what was considered a hostile village but turned into a massacre during or after the fighting. In other
instances, the troops attacked the wrong village and killed innocent
people that they had been ordered to avoid. When news of those
actions became public, it evoked sharp criticism of army leaders and
demands for peace and meaningful reforms in dealing with tribal
people.

So many massacres happened that one might argue that the practice
became a sort of unwritten military policy. However, historians looking at army campaigns against the Indians during that era have suggested that some of the massacres examined here occurred despite the
officer corps' legal and intellectual rejections of total-war tactics. They
point to the long-standing prohibition against looting civilians' goods or
their property that existed as far back as a directive in the 1806 Articles
of War stating that "any officer or soldier who shall quit his post or colors

to plunder and pillage shall suffer death or such other punishment as shall be ordered by sentence of a general court-marshal."[18]

Clearly American military leaders accepted European martial thinking at that point. They considered the practice of depriving an opposing army of its supplies to be legitimate but rejected looting or violence against civilians. Major General Henry W. Halleck, who commanded the army for much of the Civil War, agreed. During the 1840s he had spoken out clearly against troops' living off the land or attacking civilians.[19] These ideas lasted into the Civil War era: in 1863 the army issued General Order One Hundred, which stated that "the unarmed civilian is to be spared in person, property, and honor as much as the exigencies of war will allow." However, vicious guerrilla raids on army supply columns during the war and the perceived need for total Union victory changed those attitudes.[20]

Yet, unlike twentieth century wars, even when General William Tecumseh Sherman led his destructive army through Georgia and South Carolina and General Philip Henry Sheridan's forces ravaged the Shenandoah Valley, their troops rarely attacked civilians. That changed in late 1864, when both men became proponents of punitive war: their experiences persuaded them that destroying property was just as important as destroying life in bringing peace.[21] Sheridan applied this idea dramatically after the Civil War when his victorious troops moved west to engage the Indians. His men attacked villages thought to include hostile Indians in winter when the villagers had lost much of their mobility. However, the troops' actions in those campaigns went far beyond Civil War property destruction in the South. In the West they attacked villages, burned property, shot captured horses, often killed women and children, and committed physical atrocities during the fighting. Those actions signaled a policy of total war already practiced against the Indians and often a lack of firm control over the attacking troops. This study asks how, why, and when did those attacks become massacres rather than just one-sided military victories?

Generals Sherman and Sheridan, who oversaw most of these massacres, both experienced the national schizophrenia concerning Indian affairs. Critics blasted them for nearly every action they took. Western politicians and newspapers reacted to army dealings with the Indians in several ways. They attacked the military when troops failed to protect pioneer travelers or settlers from Indian raids or praised them for destroying the "savages." At the same time, eastern politicians, reformers, and media denounced the generals as butchers when the harsh measures they used went beyond simple military victory. For much of the late nineteenth century some Americans objected strongly to whatever action the troops took: public attacks on military actions and competence appeared frequently.

Much of the literature on Euro-American/Indian relations considers the violence and military actions that occurred. Biographies of tribal leaders and the army officers who directed battles as well as studies of campaigns or other army activities in the West may be found at many libraries. Military historians and scholars interested in tribal histories have produced thoughtful narratives that analyze particular massacres clearly, but rarely do they look for patterns or present an overall analysis of such events. This book examines Indian massacres by federal troops and militia forces across the country as the result of complex situations where the usual restraints against killing innocent and unarmed villagers broke down. Using existing scholarship on these incidents, this study considers the local situation in which each massacre occurred. Those varied widely but include the often violent relations between the Indians and their white neighbors, which provided motivations for repeated attacks by either side. Where possible, this book compares the results of these events.

Any study of warfare with the Indians must recognize that the tribal leaders' lack of authority to prevent their people from attacking nearby whites played a central role in the resulting violence. So did American officials' refusal to recognize or accept that reality, which left them without anyone to hold responsible. That circumstance explains why some village leaders thought that they were at peace, while military authorities treated them as being hostile. Some people might like to view these incidents as representing a kind of slaughter of the innocents, but that is far too simplistic. In nearly every case the frontier whites described their attacks against the Indians as necessary and justified responses to raids, thievery, kidnapping, and property destruction committed by tribal people. Despite those charges, the fighting that occurred resulted from the settlers' anti-Indian ideas and actions, which made life dangerous for people of both races.

Because neither the village chiefs nor American officials could or would keep peace when the two peoples met, that task devolved upon the army. It had the responsibility to prevent violence and to keep Indians and whites apart. The incidents considered here show how and why it failed and how its inability or unwillingness to avoid warfare brought massacres to many tribes during the nineteenth century. These events include all the major recognized massacres of Indians by U.S. troops during the nineteenth century. They appear in chronological order, which allows the analysis to build on similarities with earlier events. That order also mirrors American territorial expansion and western settlement patterns. Based on any reasonable definition and thoughtful analysis of the data, these incidents must all be labeled massacres. They represent the unacknowledged dishonorable side of American national expansion as whites completed their 300-year invasion of the continent.

CHAPTER 1

Red Stick War, 1813–1814

The first clear massacres of Indians committed by American troops after independence happened during the Red Stick War in Alabama. That conflict opened and closed with massacres. The first one happened during an early-morning attack on November 3, 1813, when General John Coffee's 900 mounted troops surrounded the village of Tallushatchee. The main body of attackers encircled it while two companies of men rode into the town center and retreated quickly, hoping to lure the defenders into the open. The ploy worked: Indian fighters rushed out of their lodges to drive the troops away, as Coffee had expected. Heavy fire by his troops drove the exposed Creeks back into the village. Outnumbered, and often fighting with only bows and arrows, all 186 of the defenders died that morning. Davy Crockett, serving as a militiaman, wrote that the soldiers shot the Creeks "down like dogs." He helped burn down a large building housing 46 of the warriors and their families. According to Crockett, the Red Sticks retreated to their flimsy houses: some of the wives and children and the wounded fighters died when fires spread through the village, leaving a "revolting scene," where "half consumed bodies were seen amidst the smoking ruins."[1]

The next morning another column of troops arrived, and years later one of them remembered the carnage: "it was to me a horrible and revolting scene. . . . They fought in the midst of their wives and children, who frequently shared their bloody fate. . . . We found as many as eight or ten bodies in a single cabin. . . . In [some] instances dogs had torn and feasted on the mangled bodies of their masters."[2] When news of the attack later became public knowledge, General Coffee defend the killing of women and children during the fighting. He blamed their deaths on the Creeks rather than on his troops: because the warriors had retreated to their homes, they had exposed their families to the soldiers' fire.[3]

This conflict had two basic causes. First, American frontier leaders were determined to acquire the rich Creek lands in southern Alabama. Second, a bitter civil war was tearing through the Creek Confederacy. It pitted the Red Sticks, followers of nativist prophets and opponents of acculturation taking place in some of the tribal communities, against those who had accepted American social and economic practices. Most of the Lower Creek villages objected to the new prophets' teachings and wanted no part of a possible war with the whites. Some of their leaders had close ties to American traders, which also influenced their actions. The militants hoped that the Spanish officials in Pensacola would supply them with weapons and ammunition as the British had done for tribes in the North. The Spanish hoped that the Creeks would become a shield between their weakly held outposts and the aggressive American pioneers just across the border. Eager to make that happen, in the summer of 1813 authorities in Pensacola invited Red Stick leaders to confer. The Creeks hoped that they would receive arms. When the talks ended, the disappointed Indians returned home without any new weapons. A few weeks later Peter McQueen led another group of three hundred warriors back to Florida to ask the newly arrived governor of Spanish West Florida, Mateo González Manrique, for supplies. After tense negotiations, he gave them some.[4]

On their way home McQueen's force split into smaller parties. A group of nearly two hundred Mississippi militiamen from nearby Fort Mims and a few mixed-race Lower Creeks ambushed one of the small Red Stick parties at Burnt Corn Creek in what is now Alabama. When the startled Red Sticks fled, the attackers began looting their supplies instead of following them. At that point the Indians charged out of the canebrakes, surprised and scattered their attackers, and retook the horses and baggage. Emboldened by their easy victory over the more numerous militiamen and enraged because some of their fellow tribesmen had joined the attack against them, the Red Sticks threatened many nearby settlements. In midsummer of 1813 several of their chiefs led a force of nearly a thousand men in a sweeping campaign to destroy the farms, gristmills, livestock, and plantations in the Tensaw area, where many Lower Creeks and Métis had accepted American-style agriculture. When news of the raids spread, white farmers and their Creek–Métis neighbors fled streaming into the nearby towns of Mobile and St. Stephens and to Fort Stoddard. Other Lower Creek plantation owners and local white farmers loaded their goods, families, and slaves onto flatboats and hurried down the Alabama River to join the refugees already gathered at Fort Mims, a crudely built and poorly defended stockade at the plantation home of setter Samuel Mims.[5]

On August 30, 1813, fighting between the two sides began when the Red Sticks attacked Fort Mims. That structure sheltered nearly 500 pioneers, acculturated Creeks, Métis, slaves, and some Mississippi militiamen who had fled there for protection. Seeing the refugees as an easy target and determined to destroy the Creeks and Métis who had joined the whites at Burnt Corn Creek, William Weatherford, known as Red Eagle, led nearly 750 men against the fort. Before the attack Red Stick shaman Paddy Walsh encouraged the warriors to fight, promising them protection from the defenders' weapons. The attackers burst into the fort and seized several of the buildings. After bitter hand-to-hand fighting they killed most of the defenders and burned the buildings. When the battle ended, the Indians had reduced the fort to a smoldering ruin and killed most of the 500 people. They took 100 prisoners, most of them slaves. After leaving the smoldering ruins of Fort Mims, the attackers stormed through the area, killing thousands of cattle and horses, destroying neighboring farms and plantations, and killing or stealing slaves wherever they went. Their actions fit any definition of massacre. News of their actions spread terror across the region. This bloody victory cost the Red Sticks heavy casualties, but more importantly it brought the United States into what had begun as a Creek civil war.[6] Unlike most Indian conflicts, this one included battles where hundreds of tribesmen fought rather than flee or surrender, which resulted in massive numbers of casualties from the battles.

News of the massacre at Fort Mims sparked wild rumors in nearby frontier settlements and demands for retaliation. In Washington, D.C., the Madison administration appointed Major General Thomas Pinckney to lead the American response. A hurriedly proposed plan called for two militia armies from Tennessee under General Andrew Jackson, a second militia force from Mississippi Territory, and the Third Regiment of United States Army regulars, to invade Creek territory from three directions. They had orders to assault any Red Sticks they met, attack their villages, and destroy their crops and property.[7] Like most pioneer militiamen, the troops needed little encouragement to ravage Indian villages. For many of them the indigenous people constituted a real physical threat as well as an obstacle to their new settlements. They had grown to adulthood hearing tales of Indian violence and cruelty and had little sympathy for their tribal neighbors. In the campaign that followed these units marched through Creek territory, destroying nearly fifty towns and villages, burning crops, slaughtering livestock, and most importantly killing Indians.

Despite a shortage of food for the troops and the expiration of the enlistments of many militiamen during the campaign, Jackson's force fought major battles throughout the region. Defending their land and autonomy, the lightly armed warriors fought fiercely, suffering hundreds of casualties and deaths. Jackson's army of militia, U.S. forces, and their Cherokee and Creek allies attacked nearly all the major Red Stick towns. During the hostilities at least five major battles occurred during the hostilities: at Tallushatchee, Talladega, Hillabee, Autossee, and Tohopika or Horseshoe Bend. Women and children were killed, wounded, or captured in the heavy fighting at most of these sites, while hundreds of the men died in the fighting. Those battles led to massacres of both Creek defenders and noncombatants.

The Red Stick War that began in 1813 evolved out of a long series of events that stretched back at least half a century before the fighting began. During the late colonial era, fifty or more scattered Muskogean villages in present Georgia and Alabama with nearly twenty thousand people formed the Creek Confederacy. Their villages included Yucki, Natchez, Alabama, and Shawnee migrants who joined Creek communities. To outsiders the resulting society appeared solid because the newcomers shared language and social customs, but unity proved elusive for them. Incorporating refugees into their villages brought long-term divisions within Creek society.[8] The new confederacy had little historical longevity, and few leaders recognized by more than a handful of villages. While their basic customs, economy, and shared language bound them together, they had few strong ties beyond their own local settlements. Their limited connections with other villages also meant that most tribal authority remained local, in the hands of community and band leaders rather than nationally recognized chiefs.[9] Nearby whites saw them as two distinct groups: Upper Creeks located mostly in present central Alabama and Lower Creeks in southern Alabama and in western Georgia.

During the 1763–83 era disagreements between Upper and Lower Creek chiefs about how to deal with the advancing pioneers led to growing divisions within Muskogean society, often based on whether they had American, British, or Spanish trading partners. For example, just before American independence some Upper Creek leaders objected when chiefs of Lower Creek towns signed treaties ceding large areas tribal land to Georgia.[10] The land surrenders and the continual demands from Georgia leaders for additional cessions brought persistent major stresses within Creek society. For some decades white traders had lived among the villagers, marrying women from prominent families, becoming recognized community leaders, and serving as models for a growing assimilation movement, mostly among the Lower Creek villages. This took place in the Upper Creek towns too but had less impact there.

One of these Métis leaders, the Scots-Creek Alexander McGillivray, helped to bring major but contentious changes to the confederacy. He wore white man's clothing, ignored hunting, and never became a warrior. Despite appearing to flout Creek customs, he became a recognized leader in the tribe. Objecting bitterly to Lower Creek land cessions to Georgia, he encouraged tribal chiefs to sign the Treaty of Pensacola with Spanish officials in 1784 and thereby gained access to Spanish arms and supplies. In the face of criticism McGillivray explained that he was working to help the Creeks remain "independent of the American states . . . & to preserve our Lands."[11]

With personal ties to both British and Spanish traders, McGillivray persuaded Upper Creek chiefs to support him, but Lower Creek leaders with close ties to American traders objected to his actions.[12] As a former British agent his actions angered the pro-American Lower Creek chiefs. He tried to blunt their opposition by getting support from the warrior councils by giving their members guns and ammunition.

During the 1780s Georgia authorities moved into the vacuum caused by the weak new federal government's tepid interest in Indian affairs. State leaders demanded that Lower Creek chiefs sign treaties ceding tribal land in 1783, 1785, and 1786. The Creek National Council rejected these agreements and punished one of the signers. At that point McGillivray stated that the Indians would refuse to sign any more treaties and that if the whites wanted the land they should "come and take it."[13] Following his lead, some of the chiefs rejected further Georgia demands and led raids against the settlers in the disputed area. By 1789 their attacks had persuaded the Georgians to call for negotiations between the new federal government and the tribe. At first American officials demanded that the Creeks recognize the Georgia claims, but tribal leaders refused. Then in 1790 President Washington invited Creek diplomats to New York City for talks, which resulted in their signing the Treaty of New York, a peace agreement, that year.[14]

Clearly McGillivray wanted to strengthen and unite the Creek villagers, and he tried to use the National Council to do that. Just three years after his death in 1793, Benjamin Hawkins, an American official, saw the council as a force to break down the tribal culture and help him acculturate the tribe. He tried to persuade the chiefs that they should end their dependence on hunting for the fur and hide trade and adopt American-style sedentary agriculture.[15] Hawkins established a model plantation, planted an orchard, cultivated a large vegetable garden, had fenced well-tilled fields, and kept herds of livestock. Later he added a sawmill, a grist-mill, and a blacksmith shop for the Indians' use. Before long a few of the men began raising livestock because they had killed nearly all the deer that provided food and hides for trade, but they had no intention to work in gardens or fields. That task was for the women.[16]

As he tried to change Creek society, Hawkins turned his attention to wealthy men and the National Council. He encouraged that body to extend its authority, expecting to use it to achieve his goals. Under orders to get the Creeks to accept new treaties in 1802, he persuaded them to sign the Treaty of Fort Wilkinson that year. In the negotiations Hawkins bribed several Creek chiefs to sell some of the neighboring Seminoles' best hunting land over that tribe's objections. His interference created opposition and repeatedly divided Creek leaders over their agent's actions. His activities also led to direct opposition when he asked for land for roads that would penetrate the center of Creek country. In 1811, when the National Council leaders rejected his demands, he turned to bribery to get their assent to the federal road.[17]

Some of the chiefs saw Hawkins's influence as harmful to their cultural survival and constantly objected.[18] Their competing views kept the National Council in turmoil much of the time. The council's debate over how to respond to American demands to accept a military road through Creek territory split the tribal leadership. Urging the council to reject Hawkins's demand, one chief replied: "You ask for a path and I say no. . . . I hope it will never be mentioned again."[19] The Upper Creek chiefs objected that pioneer settlers using any road through Creek country would cause trouble; some wanted to keep them out of tribal territory altogether. At the same time some Lower Creek leaders hoped to benefit from tolls collected from whites using ferries to cross the rivers and their spending at Indian-operated roadside inns.

During its 1811 debate over the proposed new federal road, the National Council hosted Shawnee diplomat and war leader Tecumseh and a delegation from the Ohio Valley tribes. The visitors had come south to recruit Indians there for a multitribal coalition against the Americans. The National Council welcomed the visitors and agreed to listen. In his address Tecumseh reminded the council members of how much land they had lost to the Americans and urged his listeners to defend their tribal independence by joining the Ohio Valley tribes in a multitribal alliance.[20]

Tecumseh tied his vision of Indian nationalism to the religious teachings of his half-brother, the Shawnee Prophet Tenskwatawa. Some of the chiefs welcomed their visitor's ideas for several reasons. Hoboithle Mico, chief of the village of Tallassee, objected to American demands for a road that would cut directly through his people's territory. Several other leaders saw Tecumseh's effort as a chance to oppose the increasing Americanization of their villages. Influential Métis leaders Josiah Francis (a popular shaman), Peter McQueen (a wealthy planter from the same village), and William Weatherford joined the effort to block further acculturation. Chiefs in some of the Lower Creek towns also supported the visitor's ideas.[21]

Tecumseh's visit had a major impact that summer because of two natural events that village shamans interpreted as spiritual omens in favor of joining him. First, late that summer a major comet appeared and was seen by most Creeks. Tecumseh's Indian name was "Shooting Star": he argued that what many Creeks saw as a marvel was spiritual support for his cause. When the comet remained bright until November, many Creeks accepted it as an omen supporting Tecumseh's anti-American ideas. The second event, the New Madrid, Missouri, earthquakes of December 11, 1811, occurred soon after he returned north to Indiana. The epicenter lay in the northeast corner of Arkansas, but the quake destroyed New Madrid. The tremors reached all the way north and east to New England. The ground had barely stopped shaking when subsequent quakes took place on January 23 and March 15, 1812. City officials in Louisville, Kentucky, reported that their community had experienced 1,874 aftershocks. The whites recognized these events as geologic activity, but the Creeks had another explanation. They remembered that Tecumseh had threatened to stamp his foot to destroy the lodges in one of the villages that refused to join his effort.[22]

The villagers' discontent with American land grabbing, cultural erosion, and settler encroachments as well as the Shawnee visitor's urgings attracted many. Some looked to their spiritual leaders for advice. Sam Isaacs, an Upper Creek shaman, reported seeing visions and receiving new religious teachings from a giant serpent that he claimed had caused some of the quakes. Other shamans reported spiritual signs too, but their specific ideas have been lost. Whatever teachings they offered, all of them objected to Hawkins's acculturation program. Some called for the Creeks to change their food sources from domestic animals to wild game and from grain and other crops to nuts and berries. But by that time Creek hunters had killed so many of the native animals that anyone who followed that advice faced starvation. When some of the religious leaders urged these changes, many of the villagers took the red sticks (painted clubs) that the men used in combat as their emblem. Calling themselves Red Sticks, they began attacking travelers on the federal road from Georgia. In the spring of 1812 they killed several pioneer families.[23]

The raids pitted the Red Sticks against the National Council, widened the gap between the Upper and Lower Creek villages, and led directly to the Red Stick or Creek War. It began during the War of 1812 and occurred in part because of that conflict. While returning south from an early 1813 visit to Tenskwatawa's village in Indiana and thinking that the Creeks had gone to war with the United States, Chief Little Warrior and his companions destroyed a small pioneer settlement near the mouth of the Ohio River. The chief described the attack proudly when he reached home, but instead of praising him the other chiefs "severely reprimanded" him and ordered him out of the council house. The council decided to punish Little Warrior and sent more than a hundred men to kill him and his companions. They murdered all but one of the band, who had fled.[24]

That action shattered the fragile unity within the Creek Confederacy. By the summer of 1813 a full-scale civil war had erupted. The Red Stick prophets urged their followers to "[k]ill the old chiefs, [who were] friends to peace."[25] On the surface it looks as if the conflict followed the lines of class and acculturation: the more traditional groups opposed the successful ranchers, plantation owners, and small business owners. However, rather than reflecting class-based divisions, the war became a rebellion against the growing American threat to tribal culture and the actions of the National Council. Some prominent wealthy Creeks joined the rebellion. For example, despite being acculturated and economically successful, Josiah Francis, Peter McQueen, and William Weatherford joined traditionalists such as Hoboithle Mico and High Head Jim by becoming Red Stick leaders. Other unidentified shamans and traditional chiefs joined the movement too.[26] The war also highlighted the differing allegiances with American, British, and Spanish traders and officials that separated the Upper and Lower Creek towns.

Once fighting between the United States and Britain began in 1812, federal leaders worried that Spanish officers in the South would encourage and supply tribes there as the British did from Canada in the North. That potential threat never materialized, because Spanish authorities lacked the resources and the will to incite the southern tribes to fight against the Americans. Despite that hesitancy, in the summer of 1813 Spanish officials in Pensacola invited Red Stick leaders for talks. The Indians hoped that their hosts would offer them new weapons and ammunition, but that did not happen. Instead the Spanish wanted to make long-term plans for the area. When the talks ended, they sent the Creeks home empty-handed. Many of the Red Stick men had only bows and arrows or war clubs, so Peter McQueen soon led a group of three hundred warriors back to Pensacola to plead for weapons. The governor gave them gunpowder, lead, food, and blankets but no new guns.[27]

As McQueen's followers returned home, frontier militiamen and a few Lower Creeks attacked them at Burnt Corn Creek. The enraged Red Sticks began a full-scale civil war by attacking Fort Mims, which in turn led to the Creek War with the United States. After the fighting at Fort Mims, Andrew Jackson led at least two thousand Tennessee militiamen south into Alabama Territory. Before they marched south, he encouraged the troops to eliminate Indians from the area so that "the soil which now lies waste and uncultivated may be converted into rich harvest fields, to supply the wants of millions."[28] Few hesitated to follow his urging.

General Coffee's destruction of Tallushatchee in November 1813 persuaded the Creeks opposing the Red Sticks rebellion to ask Andrew Jackson for help. They sent a messenger telling him that William Weatherford (Red Eagle) with more than eight hundred or nine hundred men had surrounded them at Fort Leslie, a palisaded trading post near the village of Talladega. Responding quickly on November 9, 1813, Jackson led a force of nearly two thousand men to break the siege. They surrounded the fort and its attackers and began firing. After the fight Davy Crockett wrote that the Indians "came rushing forth . . . like all the young devils had been turned loose" to defend themselves.[29] During the battle the militiamen's fire killed three hundred of the Red Sticks, but Weatherford and nearly seven hundred more men escaped when one of the militia units retreated instead of advancing at a crucial moment.[30] This time the only noncombatants at the scene were those seeking shelter at Fort Leslie, who seem not to have suffered any casualties.

The American victories at Tallushatchee and Talladega persuaded some of the Red Sticks to drop out of the war, and the Hillabee people, who had suffered major losses in the two defeats, asked Jackson for peace. He agreed and on November 17, 1813, granted it. That action led directly to the worst atrocity in the war. Just a day after the Hillabee villagers dropped out of the fighting General Hugh White, unaware of Jackson's promise of peace, attacked at least three Hillabee towns. Because the villagers had just signed a peace agreement, they had no idea that other troops might attack them. The assault by White's men caught them totally unprepared, so they could offer little more than token resistance. In the attack the militiamen entirely destroyed two of the smaller villages, apparently killing nearly everyone there: they mentioned no survivors and took no prisoners. When the fighting ended, they burned all the dwellings in each town. Then they attacked, defeated, and captured those living at the undefended larger Hillabee village, killing 60 and capturing another 250 people. Following that "battle," they bragged that "we lost not a drop of blood." Having just agreed to peace with Jackson, the Hillabees felt betrayed and became some of the most bitterly anti-American of the Red Stick fighters.[31] Few details of this incident exist, but the entire destruction of two unarmed villages and the attack on the third village clearly constituted one of the largest massacres in early American history.

During the 1813–14 winter Jackson's army almost melted away as the troops' short-term enlistments began to end; supply shortages plagued the troops. Despite that, the general fought two battles with the Red Sticks, barely surviving the second one. Once new militia units and more U.S. troops arrived, Jackson moved his force near the large Red Stick village at a place that the Indians called the Horse's Flat Foot, Horseshoe Bend to the whites. This peninsula of nearly a hundred acres, with the river on three sides, had a well-built log palisade across its narrow neck, described as being "from five to eight feet high." Its builders had cut "double rows of portholes" that allowed the defenders to shoot attackers who tried to get close to the stockade. Apparently the nine hundred or so villagers there assumed that they were safe because of their log defense and the whites' inability to get across the river easily.[32]

In late March 1814 Jackson led a force that combined several thousand militiamen with six hundred soldiers of the 39th Regiment and five hundred Cherokee and one hundred Creek allies, against an estimated one thousand Red Stick fighters and their families then in the fortified village at Horseshoe Bend. The whites crossed the river and moved to encircle the village, blocking any possible escape. At that point some their Indian allies attacked the village from the rear, while others swam across the river and took many of the canoes that the Creeks had left on the bank. They brought them back across the river and used them to move more fighters to the end of the peninsula.

At first, Jackson used his two small cannons to break through the log stockade, but most of the shots bounced off the log defenses. Seeing that his artillery was ineffective, he ordered a frontal assault: the attackers swarmed to the wall. Some fired through the portholes that the defenders had been using while others clamored over the palisade. As Jackson's men rushed into the village, the Red Sticks refused to surrender, despite being outnumbered by about three to one and not having as many good weapons as their enemies. When he realized that his troops controlled the battlefield, the general tried to end the fighting. He sent several officers and interpreters with an offer of peace if the Indians surrendered, but the fighting resumed when the Red Sticks killed or wounded several of the men.[33]

Some of the Red Sticks fought to protect their families huddled in their lodges, but others tried to escape by swimming across the river. There they became targets for the cavalrymen and Indian allies who lined the opposite shore. One of the battle reports stated that despite their "attempts to cross the river . . . not one ever escaped, very few reached the bank and that few was killed the instant they landed." Jackson disclosed that "the enemy . . . were at length entirely routed and cut to pieces. The whole margin [bank] of the river . . . was strewn with the slain."[34]

So many men died on the riverbank or while trying to cross it that one of the militiamen claimed that the bloody water stained his horse almost up to its shoulders when he rode through the river. Because the soldiers and their Indian allies had surrounded the Red Stick village, only about 20 Red Sticks survived the slaughter. That meant that about 900 Creek fighters died in the battle. Jackson's force suffered 131 men killed or wounded in the fighting.[35] The Cherokees and Lower Creeks who aided Jackson's force fought to retaliate for perceived wrongs that the Creek defenders had committed earlier. Their participation certainly was part of the indiscriminate killing that took place during the battle.

The victorious troops committed atrocities as well as killing noncombatants and Creek fighters. One militiaman clubbed a five-year-old boy to death with his musket, defending his action because the boy would grow up and become a warrior, the same reasoning used in later battles fought farther west. Another soldier shot an old man sitting beside one of the lodges so that he would have a story about his combat experience to tell. While prowling among the corpses some of the militiamen cut long strips of skin from the backs of the dead warriors to make bridle reins. To get an accurate body count the troops cut off the tips of the noses of the bodies of the dead warriors who had not been washed away by the river current.[36] General Jackson gave the surviving three hundred women and children to his Cherokee and Creek allies, who took them to their home villages. In typical Indian practice, they adopted those who were not exchanged later. With so many of their men dead, the Red Sticks ended the fighting. Groups of the most anti-American warriors fled south into Spanish Florida to begin new villages or join the groups of neighboring Seminoles beyond the nation's southern border.

The Red Stick War differs from many white/Indian conflicts because the Red Sticks chose to fight standup battles with the invading Americans. In most of the battles Jackson's forces attacked their villages, endangering the women and children, who had no chance to escape the carnage. The statistics of deaths are incomplete, and perhaps incorrect, particularly because few if any Creek accounts of the fighting have survived. Nevertheless, Jackson's invading force killed nearly two thousand Creek men, who died defending their homes from the invaders. During this campaign, the mixed force of militiamen and U.S. soldiers attacked and mostly destroyed at least fifty Red Stick Upper Creek towns, burned crops, and killed Indian-owned livestock. The civilian casualties occurred during direct attacks on the villages, because the troops made no effort to differentiate between fighting men and others and because the Red Sticks often chose to fight to the last man. Nevertheless, killing unarmed men who tried to swim across the river while fleeing the battle might well be considered a massacre.

The number of noncombatants killed or wounded in the fighting throughout this war is almost impossible to determine. However, the attacks on the Hillabee Creek towns stand out as being particularly deadly for civilians. Because they had negotiated a peace with Andrew Jackson just a day earlier, the troops found the Creeks nearly defenseless. General White's force reported that it had destroyed two of the three villages entirely and mentioned no prisoners or other survivors. By any definition that action constituted a massacre, an early example of many to follow in the process of eliminating Indians from the nation.

Because the Red Stick War was only a small part of American military actions during the War of 1812 it received less national attention than many other Indian conflicts in the early nineteenth century. Most information about the fighting came from Andrew Jackson's correspondence and official reports to his superiors and later from Davy Crockett's autobiography. By the time it appeared, few Americans knew or remembered much about this war. For those who did the events likely seemed to be part of the triumph of American civilization over Indian "savagery" that was so prevalent in the society at the time. Certainly, few knowledgeable people would have considered civilian deaths caused by attacks on Red Stick villages to be massacres. Yet those fights followed the experiences of frontier militia units in the Ohio Valley war of the 1790s. They added to the pattern set by pioneer raiders when they came to Indian villages in Ohio and Indiana: they had destroyed crops, looted Indian lodges, and killed or captured the inhabitants. No witness recorded any obvious massacres, but certainly women, children, and old people died during the fighting. By 1815 Americans had become accustomed to accounts of Indian wars as well-deserved victories. Few appear to have given any thought to the death and destruction in indigenous communities or to have seen the carnage as including massacres.

CHAPTER 2

Bad Axe, 1832

On August 1, 1832, the exhausted survivors of the British Band of Sauk Indians stumbled down through the hills to the Mississippi River. As they searched frantically for canoes or other ways to cross the river, the steamboat *Warrior* came into view. The fugitives raised a white flag as they tried to surrender, but the steamer's crew had no translator. Suspecting an Indian ambush, they opened fire with an artillery piece, killing twenty-three of the Sauks as they stood on the riverbank. When the boat turned south to refuel for the next day, some of the Sauk and Meskwakie women tried to swim or paddle across the Mississippi on small logs. Many drowned before reaching the Iowa shore.[1]

At sunup the next morning General Henry Atkinson's infantrymen and units of mounted Illinois militiamen swarmed down the hillsides near the river, trapping the remnants of the British Band at the water's edge. The soldiers and militiamen, numbering over 1,000, found the fugitive Indians there. Only about 150 Indian men remained to defend the women and children. As the soldiers attacked from land, the *Warrior* returned, raking the defenders with cannon shot from the river. As the fighting raged, Indian women tried to save their children, carrying them in blankets while swimming to safety. Some tried to hide underwater, with only their noses above the surface, but the Menominee warriors onboard the steamer shot them. During the one-sided battle, the troops needlessly killed all of the men and nearly all the boys, even when they tried to surrender.

When the firing ended, the soldiers had killed at least 150 of the British Band, while another 110 died trying to escape across the river. Perhaps 200 managed to swim across to Iowa, but Dakota Sioux auxiliaries killed many of the starving survivors.[2] During the fighting some of the volunteers purposely shot women and children, while others joined their Indian allies in hacking off the scalps of the dead warriors. The more bloodthirsty militiamen cut strips of flesh and skin from the corpses to make razor straps. As one of Colonel Henry Dodge's men remembered, "We killed everything that didn't surrender," including "three squaws [who] were naked" in the water. In defending their actions when accused of atrocities, one of the volunteers responded angrily that "we have been accused of inhumanity to those Indians. It is false as hell, we never did it!"[3]

Except for the results and the final massacre, the Black Hawk War of 1832 differed substantially from the earlier Red Stick conflict. True, the Sauks and Meskwakies had deep divisions within their village societies, but these differences had not descended into a tribal civil war as it had for the Creeks. The midwestern villagers encountered no resident agent resembling Benjamin Hawkins, who had led the settler colonial effort to acculturate the Creeks a generation earlier. Their divisions resulted from having to deal with threats from other Indians and whites rather than from fighting with each other. Sauk and Meskwakie beliefs lacked the intense nativistic religious underpinnings that motivated the Red Stick movement and its divisive impact. While the Red Sticks gathered arms and ammunition and used them in fighting major battles with U.S. forces, Black Hawk's 1832 followers did not expect a war. When fighting began, they stumbled into it by accident.

Despite these basic differences, the two conflicts shared elements present in many Indian-white conflicts. In both cases indigenous leaders hoped to secure aid and support from foreign neighbors. The Creeks tried to get materials and weapons from the Spanish authorities in Florida, while the Sauks and Meskwakies hoped for help from the British in Canada. In both cases the Indians' actions constituted responses to colonial settler pressures on their land and economic resources. Pioneer Georgians represented the major local threat to the Creek villages, while frontier lead miners and would-be farmers brought stress and discord to

the Sauks and Meskwakies. Treaties with the United States both disrupted indigenous groups and caused friction with the Americans and
within the village societies. In both conflicts American forces used Indian
auxiliaries to find and defeat their foes. These men used the wars to get
personal and tribal revenge on their enemies. In the days immediately
surrounding the Battle of Bad Axe they contributed to the slaughter of
unarmed civilians while they and their white allies committed grisly
atrocities against the losers.

The Black Hawk War erupted in 1832 after nearly three decades of
tension and mutual distrust between the indigenous communities and
the incoming pioneers. Their first dealings with the Americans came in
1804, shortly after the United States completed the Louisiana Purchase
from France. Spanish officials had directed affairs at St. Louis up to that
point. For the Indians this meant that "we should lose our Spanish
father" or trading partner. The Sauks worried about their future "because
we had always heard bad accounts of the Americans from Indians who
lived near them."[4] Incoming American officials had similar negative
views of the Sauks and Meskwakies. When taken together, these people
represented one of the largest Indian groups in the upper Mississippi
Valley. At first the Indians made no effort to begin a new relationship
with the newcomers. In fact, Captain Amos Stoddard, the American officer at St. Louis, complained that "the Sauks . . . do not pay that respect to
the United States which is entertained by the other Indians—and in
some instances they have assumed a pretty elevated tone."[5]

Despite the captain's concern, the Indians faced far more danger than
did their new neighbors. From the start the new authorities took steps to
dominate the villagers and reduce their autonomy. American policy was
aimed at persuading them to abandon their indigenous customs and
make way for the incoming pioneers. Through a questionable 1804 treaty
the United States seized tribal land. Later negotiations sought to end
culturally based retaliatory intertribal raiding and to disrupt long-
established trading patterns with British traders operating out of Canada. In 1811 and again in 1817 the army located garrisons in tribal
territory, seen as threatening or at least disrupting the villagers' day-to-
day activities. Pioneer settlers menaced the Indians too. In 1811 they
tried to occupy Meskwakie lead-bearing lands in northeastern Iowa.
Eleven years later, with government help and over vigorous objections,

they occupied the lead-rich area in southwestern Wisconsin and north-western Illinois. In 1829 white farmers moved into the village of Sauke-nuk, the Sauks' major village, taking their homes and rich farmland. These actions left Sauk and Meskwakie societies badly divided and eco-nomically weakened and resulted in their accidental drift into war.[6]

American actions in 1804 set the tone and created the situation that brought war three decades later. Acting under orders from Washington to be "particularly attentive" to the Osage tribe, considered to be a dan-gerous enemy by Sauk and Meskwakie chiefs, Captain Stoddard gave the Osage chiefs many presents. To make matters worse, U.S. officers at St. Louis intercepted and turned back a 300-man Sauk-Meskwakie war party on its way to attack the Osages. Next American authorities negoti-ated a purchase of Illinois land from the Kaskaskia Tribe: land that both the Sauks and the Kickapoos assumed was theirs. In doing so the United States rejected their claims and angered chiefs in both tribes. In fact, rumors spread that the Sauk had sent a "speech with wampum" to one Kickapoo village calling for a war to drive pioneer squatters off their land in Illinois. A Kickapoo observer reported that the messengers rode around the village, dragging an American flag from the tail of one of their horses during their visit.[7]

These strained relations might have eased over time, but four young Sauks attacked a small white settlement on tribal land near the Quivre River in Missouri. They killed three people in what the pioneers described as "a most barbarous manner," "leaving the corpses with their scalps taken off."[8] Then they rode home and threw the fresh scalps on the ground in front of the village chiefs. Taunting the tribal council "to go cry to the whites," the raiders hoped to force their leaders to move quickly against the Americans.[9]

Fearing white retaliation, the chiefs acted quickly to move several small villages farther north, away from the angry pioneers. Then they sent two chiefs and a trusted trader as interpreter to St. Louis to settle the matter. While meeting with Major James Bruff, the Sauks admitted that several of their young men had committed the murders and defended their action as retaliation for occupying unceded tribal hunting land and rumored unwanted pioneer sexual advances toward Sauk women.[10] The major demanded that the chiefs surrender the murderers and sent the men home.

Hoping to avoid war, tribal leaders sent a small delegation to St. Louis to negotiate a settlement. They surrendered one of the murderers and worked to get him released and to make peace with the United States. Unfortunately for them, the Indian delegates arrived at the same as Indiana territorial governor William Henry Harrison. As the government's chief negotiator with Indian tribes at the time, he used their meetings to extract a cession of all Sauk and Meskwakie land east of the Mississippi. Quashquame, a minor Sauk chief who led the visitors, later protested that his party never agreed to sell any tribal land but had only signed a peace agreement. It was entirely possible that they considered American claims similar to earlier French and British proclamations of political sovereignty over the area. In any case, they had no authority to cede tribal land. Given their continuing insistence that they never sold any, it appears likely that Harrison chose not to explain what the Treaty of 1804 actually meant. Whatever occurred during the 1804 St. Louis talks, the resulting treaty caused repeated misunderstandings, friction, and uncertainty for U.S.-tribal relations in the upper Mississippi Valley.[11]

The Treaty of 1804 created the Sauk anger and suspicion in regard to the United States for the next thirty years. It stood at the center of repeated disputes and misunderstandings between the villagers and their white neighbors, traders, and agents, while fueling anti-American actions such as joining the British during the War of 1812. At the same time, the agreement seemed to meet some of the tribe's immediate needs. It assured peace with the United States. The chiefs thought that Article 4 reserved their Illinois land when it promised that the government "would never interrupt the said tribes in the possession of their lands which they rightfully claim." Article 7 seemed to reinforce this idea by stating that as long as the land remained U.S. property the Indians "shall enjoy the privilege of living and hunting on them."[12] For years the chiefs thought that this guaranteed their right to live in their existing villages because the area was a part of the United States. They had no idea that American land policy assumed that the government would sell the land to pioneers. Once that happened, it would no longer belong to the government: the Indians' right to live and hunt on it would end.

While that possibility lay in the future, other American actions disrupted relations between the United States and the villagers. Continuing intertribal raiding persuaded authorities to station troops in the area, so in 1808 they sent a detachment of soldiers to begin work on Fort Madison on the west side of the Mississippi north of St. Louis. Curious, the Sauks soon learned that the troops intended to build a fort, which they saw as an invasion of their homeland during peacetime. White authorities had promised to build a government factory or fur trading post for them, but now the warriors saw only troops and weapons at the site. When village spokesmen objected, the officers replied that they were there to protect the government trader and his goods, none of which had yet arrived. That explanation failed to calm the Indians' fears about what seemed an invasion of their land, so on September 5, 1808, they tried to capture the partially built fort. They rushed toward the open gate but failed to surprise the guards. The soldiers threatened them with a loaded cannon, so the Indians withdrew.[13]

Three years later the tribes met another threat, this time to their economic well-being. Would-be white miners tried to occupy the Meskwakies' rich lead lands in northeastern Iowa at Dubuque's mines. Thirty years earlier several of the chiefs had leased some of the lead lands there to Julien Dubuque with the understanding that the claim ended if Dubuque died or left the area. Despite his agreement with the Indians, the Frenchman got title to the mining lands from Spanish officials in St. Louis. When he died in 1810, his heirs sold his presumed land rights to American investors. They hired sixty men and sent them north to reopen the mines. When the Sauks and Meskwakies heard of the miners' plans, they intercepted their boats, refused to allow them to land, and threatened to kill all of them. Their agent Nicholas Boilvin hurried to negotiate a settlement, which allowed Dubuque's heirs to remove and sell the mining equipment and let the miners leave safely. Once that happened, the Meskwakie chiefs had the buildings at the mining site burned and swore "never to give up their land until all were dead."[14]

U.S. bungling brought a second perceived attack on the tribes' economic life. Both depended on the fur trade for a major part of their annual income. An 1804 estimate stated that the Sauk trade with the Spanish had been valued at $40,000 each year, while the Meskwakies had earned about half that amount every year.[15] In early 1812 American officials hoped to keep the upper Mississippi Valley tribes neutral as the United States drifted into the War of 1812. To do that William Clark, superintendent of Indian Affairs in the area, led a delegation of chiefs to

Washington, D.C., for meetings with President James Madison. There the president told his visitors that the United States wanted them to "hunt and support their families, rather than to fight." During the meeting, the chiefs understood their host to promise that the government factor (federal fur trader) would supply them "on credit, as the British had done."[16] Either the president misunderstood their request or they received an incorrect translation of his comments, because by law the factor could not provide either alcohol or credit, both essential items in the Indian trade.

When the delegation returned home, the Indians prepared for their fall hunt. To get the supplies they needed they traveled to Fort Madison and asked the factor for the credit that they thought the president had promised. Their request surprised the trader, who responded that he could not give them any. Confused and angry, the chiefs protested that only a few weeks earlier the president had assured them that they could have credit. But the officers at the fort told their visitors that they had no orders to do that. The yearly fur trade cycle had depended on traders' giving the Indians supplies for the winter hunt, which the villagers repaid with furs and hides the next spring. The Sauks "left the fort dissatisfied" and went home. Later Black Hawk reported that they spent hours discussing what to do during a sleepless night "of gloom and discontent[ment]." Edward La Gouthrie, a long-time British trader, arrived. To the Indians' relief he brought two boats loaded with presents and supplies and invited the villagers to his camp. There he lavished presents on them and said that the British had sent the material, promising to give the hunters credit and urging Black Hawk to recruit men to join the British in fighting against the United States.[17]

The trader knew his audience well and tapped into their latent anti-American feelings. Black Hawk, in particular, had a history of such views that dated back at least to the 1804 transfer of Louisiana from Spain to the United States. Later he recalled that he "had not discovered one good trait in the character of the Americans. . . . They made fair promises but never fulfilled them! Whilst the British made but few—but we could always reply on their word."[18] The trader's presents and his offer of desperately needed credit persuaded the war leader to bring several hundred Sauk and Meskwakie men north to Green Bay. From there they joined the British and fought alongside them during the rest of the war. While they had only a modest impact on the conflict, their absence from their chief village of Saukenuk brought a major change to the leadership dynamics there.

During their absence in late 1813, Missouri and Illinois militiamen raided nearby villages. News of a threatened attack on the village with so many of the fighting men absent frightened the chiefs. They discussed moving west across the Mississippi. Hearing this proposal, young Keokuk volunteered to lead the village defenders if an attack came. None did, but his apparent bravery persuaded the chiefs to name him as the war leader in Black Hawk's absence. When the older and more experienced Black Hawk returned, the two men became heated rivals for leadership. A few years later William Clark learned of the rivalry. Seeing Keokuk as easier to dominate than the recalcitrant Black Hawk, he began giving him presents to use in gaining influence within the village. This sharpened the competition between the two men and weakened the tribe by dividing the leaders over how best to deal with the Americans.[19]

By late 1813 Black Hawk and his fellow tribesmen had left their British allies and returned home. The next spring continuing small-scale military activity kept the war active in the region. In May 1814 a small American force reached Prairie du Chien, but the British and Indians quickly recaptured the fort there. In July authorities in St. Louis sent three keelboats of militiamen north to reoccupy the post, but Sauks, Meskwakies, Ho-Chunks, and Dakota Sioux successfully attacked them. They captured one of the boats and killed many of the troops. This defeat prompted a retaliatory expedition in September 1814, led by Major Zachary Taylor. The troops on this eight-boat flotilla, larger and better armed, expected to sail past the Sauk village and then return downstream at night for a morning surprise attack. While Taylor's 320 men did pass Saukenuk, the British had sent a detachment of men with three artillery pieces and joined the multitribal attack on Taylor's men. Caught by surprise, and under heavy fire, the defeated Americans had to flee downstream, leaving the victorious Indians unimpressed with U.S. military skills.[20]

Because they had defeated Americans twice in 1814, the Sauks rejected calls to attend talks leading to the Treaty of Portage des Sioux a year later. William Clark had to issue repeated threats to attack in order to get them to sign that agreement the next year. That treaty included a Sauk acknowledgment of the earlier 1804 land cession and brought a grudging acceptance of peace in the region. For the next fifteen years no overt hostility between the native people and the invading pioneers took place. Yet ethnic tensions remained, as U.S. authorities acted in ways that limited the Indians' customs and their economy. By then the Indian societies in the area faced declining income from hunting and trade. As white settlers took up land, tribal hunters had to travel further west onto land claimed by the Pawnees and Dakota Sioux for their summer hunts. The same pressures increased rivalries with neighboring Ho-Chunks and Menominees closer to home. This competition for resources increased intertribal raiding and violence, raising American fears that the raids might trigger an regional multitribal war and endanger pioneer settlers. Hoping to prevent that, the War Department moved aggressively to secure the frontier, beginning in 1816. That year troops established Fort Edwards and Fort Armstrong in Illinois and Fort Crawford at Prairie du Chien in Wisconsin. In 1817 they built Fort Smith, Arkansas, and in 1819 erected Fort Snelling at Minneapolis/St. Paul and Fort Atkinson near present Omaha.[21]

Fort Armstrong, built on Rock Island near Saukenuk, disrupted the Indians' seclusion. Located virtually in their front yard, the new post upset village life from the start. It brought troops so close that the soldiers became nearly impossible to avoid. Black Hawk saw the new installation as one more reason to distrust the Americans. While the tribe had just signed a peace treaty with the United States, now it looked as if the whites had begun "to prepare for war in times of peace." The fort's presence angered the Indians for several reasons. It stood on a favorite summer picnic area on the nearby island. In addition the island held a spiritual significance for the villagers. They believed that a good spirit shaped like a swan lived in a small cave almost at the gate of the fort and that the soldiers had frightened it away. Black Hawk complained that when the spirit left "no doubt a bad spirit has taken its place."[22]

Although the military presence in their country played a role in dispossessing the tribes, new treaty negotiations for tribal land for the United States remained a central part of the process of replacing Indians with white settlers. Treaty talks reopened in 1816 when Ottawa, Pottawatomi, and Ojibwa chiefs surrendered their vague claims to the lead-rich area where Wisconsin, Illinois, and Iowa meet along the Mississippi. The region clearly belonged to the Meskwakies, Sauks, and Ho-Chunks who lived there and mined the lead. Ignoring their strong claims, Washington

bureaucrats signed leases giving white miners the right to begin operations there. In 1822 the secretary of war ordered agents Thomas Forsythe and Nicholas Boilvin to warn the Indians that the miners would
soon move into the Fever River area in northwestern Illinois, near present Galena.[23]

Meskwakie chiefs immediately protested against this direct attack on
their economic base and echoed Black Hawk's words, saying that they
had never sold any of their land north of the mouth of the Rock River.
Forsythe recognized the Indians' fears and commented that "I cannot
see how the major part of the Foxes [Meskwakies] and some of the Sauk
could exist without those mines."[24] He was correct, because by then the
Indians were selling thousands of dollars' worth of lead at St. Louis to
replace their shrinking income from the fur trade. The agent suggested
that the Meskwakies shift their mining west across the Mississippi to
avoid having conflicts with the newly arriving white miners. The chiefs
rejected his advice and told him that they would lease some of their Illinois land to the government, to recoup some of the income that they
would lose by leaving the Illinois lead area. The agent had no choice but
to reject their proposal, repeating the government's stand that the 1804
and 1816 treaties had ceded the disputed land to the United States. He
warned the chiefs that if they continued to object, or threatened the
miners, they would face military punishment.[25] Within a few weeks after
this meeting several thousand miners swarmed into the area.

Having occupied the villagers' neighborhood and undercut their economic well-being by reducing their lead mining, American officials refo-
cused their attention on their efforts to change native practices of
governance and diplomacy. This effort had begun with the Treaty of
1804, which called for an end to the deeply entrenched custom of exact-
ing clan revenge for injuries to persons or property in the village. That
practice included diplomacy to "cover the blood" through payments or
other means satisfactory to both sides. The treaty stated that "for injuries
done by individuals no private revenge or retaliation shall take place" but
that the injured parties should report the matter to American officials,
who would settle the matter.[26] The treaty demanded that village chiefs
surrender people accused of crimes by whites to American authorities,
This called for them to exercise an arrest power that they lacked, forced
them to anger frontier officials by not complying with those demands,

and struck directly at customary clan obligations that called for revenge for injuries.

To reinforce the treaty demands, American officials took tribal chiefs to Washington, D.C., repeatedly. They hoped that after seeing the size of eastern cities village leaders would give up any idea of resistance and would cooperate. Following continued violence among the upper Mississippi Valley tribes, in 1824 William Clark led a delegation of chiefs east, hoping to achieve peace. At the capital Keokuk, now recognized as the principal spokesman for the Sauks, met secretary of war John C. Calhoun for talks about the tribe's land claims. Keokuk objected to the American purchase of land in Missouri that the Sauks considered theirs and to pioneers' incursions on the tribe's hunting land there. When Calhoun explained that the government had bought the land from the Osages, Keokuk rejected that action. He told his host that the area belonged to the Sauks and that they had acquired it the same way the United States got land: they took it from their enemies by force.[27]

Unhappy with what they saw as unequal and unfair treatment by the Americans, Sauk and Meskwakie leaders looked north to their traditional allies, the British. In this way their actions resembled those of the Red Sticks, who had looked south across the border hoping for help from the Spanish. The tribes of the upper Mississippi Valley area had long established good relations with traders and frontier military and Indian officers from Canada. During the War of 1812, many of them had fought alongside British troops against the Americans. By the 1820s hundreds of villagers from the area made annual visits to Fort Amherst at Malden, Ontario, just across the river from Detroit. So many people made the summer trip that their route became known as the Great Sauk Trail. Their hosts welcomed them, offered presents and advice, and cautioned them about anti-American actions. They warned their visitors that Britain and the United States were at peace: if they stumbled into a war with the Americans, they could not expect any help from north of the border.[28] Despite that plain talk, some of the visitors continued to hope for British support in the face of increasing American pressures.

While U.S. frontier officers worked to keep peace and weaken tribal customs during the mid-1820s, the increasing numbers of miners attracted merchants and farmers to the area. Their presence led to frequent minor misunderstandings and incidents between the pioneers and the intruding whites. Both sides complained of damaged or lost property and livestock, theft, personal insults, and violence. The settlers, often too lazy to fence their fields, blamed bands of Indians for their missing animals, while Indians reported having whites take their horses and guns and complained of beatings by frontier thugs.[29] These often violent meetings kept both whites and Indians on edge and encouraged village malcontents as they opposed the peace chiefs' efforts to deal with the Americans.

Competition and violence involving nearby tribes added to the difficulties with their white neighbors and kept frontier officials tense. For example, despite the multitribal agreement in the Treaty of 1825 to keep hunting parties off lands claimed by other tribes, village leaders could not enforce the agreement. When Sauk hunters reported a large Dakota Sioux band camping on their land in Iowa in 1827, Black Hawk and Meskwakie leader Morgan both demanded that village chiefs take some action. When they failed to do so, the two dissidents began recruiting men to attack the Sioux. The chiefs worked to persuade the two men to stay at peace, offering Black Hawk seven horses and other presents, but he refused. Realizing that their effort had failed, the chiefs appealed to agent Forsyth for help. He, in turn, notified the Sioux agent of the planned attack and threatened to arrest Black Hawk and the others and take them in chains to St. Louis. Once the war party leaders realized that the Sioux had learned of their plan, they abandoned it, fearing a Sioux ambush.[30] This incident showed the growing split among leaders in the two tribes between the peace chiefs (who believed that survival demanded that they avoid violence) and dissidents, who came to be known as the British Band.

When increasing American pressures weakened the two tribes' economies, and interfered with their diplomatic practices, some of the villagers turned to religion for guidance. Unlike the Red Sticks, who experienced a major religious revival led by several shamans, some of the Sauks and Meskwakies turned to a mixed-blood Sauk/Ho-Chunk shaman named Wabokieshiek or White Cloud, often called the Winnebago Prophet. He led a small multitribal village and had some influence among nearby Sauk, Meskwakie, and Ho-Chunk villagers. After they met for the first time in 1827 agent Forsyth reported that he had promised to work for peace.[31] When Black Hawk and the British Band leaders asked for advice several years later, he told them that the whites would allow them to live on their land east of the Mississippi if they remained peaceful. That promise helped persuade some unhappy villagers to join the 1832 return to Illinois, leading directly to war that summer.

The ongoing contacts between Indians and Illinois pioneers increased dramatically in 1829 when the General Land Office placed the land at Saukenuk up for public auction. Following their usual practice, prior to the land sale settlers squatted illegally on choice plots, particularly those at or near the Indian village. They arrived in early spring just before the Indians returned from their winter hunt, tore down the lodges, fenced many of the well-tended fields, planted crops on what had been Sauk land, and demanded that Forsyth protect them from Indian threats. In response the villagers objected to what they saw as the theft of their land and destruction of their homes and complained to the agent that the whites had robbed them of some of their horses, rifles, tools, and blankets. Forsyth replied that he had no authority to remove the pioneers. He reminded the Indians of the 1804 treaty that sold their land and urged them to join their relatives west of the Mississippi.[32] They refused, and violent incidents continued during the summer.

Despite their agent's urgings that they remain west of the Mississippi, the villagers returned in 1830 and again the next year. White settlers with legal title to the land repeatedly complained about what they saw as an Indian invasion. In early summer of 1831 General Edmund P. Gaines arrived, leading six companies of federal troops. He confronted the Sauk leaders and told them that they had three days to cross the Mississippi or he would force them to do so. The villagers objected, but he was adamant. When several hundred Illinois mounted volunteers arrived, Black Hawk and the other leaders protested that they lacked enough food to survive the winter. The general agreed to supply them. At that point they agreed to leave what was left of their village. Local observers expected that this settled the issue and that the malcontents would stay west of the river. They misjudged the Indians' determination to stay in their village.[33]

While frontier officials hoped that they had ended the problems, pioneers dug up Indian graves at Saukenuk, exhumed some of the remains, and burned the bones. Hearing this, infuriated Indians returned to the village to rebury the dead, but armed whites drove them way. A few weeks later some of the women returned to harvest the corn that they had planted, only to be driven away by armed settlers again.[34] At this point the hard-core opponents of abandoning Saukenuk began to attract those with other motivations. They gradually united into what became known incorrectly as the British Band. Pioneers gave them that name because of their annual visits to Malden to hold councils with British officials there. In addition to those who wanted to remain at their Rock River village, the group included people who disliked Keokuk's leadership and the civil chiefs' cooperation with the Americans.

Others had joined the British Band by early 1832 for a variety of reasons. The 1830 Sioux and Menominee murder of an unarmed Meskwakie peace delegation angered many in that tribe. When the United States failed to punish the killers, they joined the British Band.[35] Indian women who had been forced west into Iowa had practical complaints. They found that their digging sticks failed to cut through the thick Iowa sod, making it nearly impossible to prepare their new fields for planting, and that they had lost access to the groves of maple trees where they went to make sugar each spring. The men used arguments based on masculinity and patriotism. When Keokuk had advised the villagers to leave their Illinois home, Black Hawk denounced him bitterly. "I looked upon him as a coward, and no brave, to abandon his village to be occupied by strangers," he recalled.[36] While the refugees huddled around their fires during the 1831–32 winter, wild rumors swept through their camps. One described a plan to take all of the Indian men, "young and old, and deprive them of those parts which are said to be *essential* to courage." Connected to the threat to castrate the men came the story that having done that the government would then bring in "a horde of Negro men . . . to whom our wives, sisters, and daughters were to be given, for the purpose of raising a stock of *Slaves* to supply the demand of the country."[37]

There is no way to know whether these rumors persuaded any people to join the British Band. Estimates vary as to how many people it included when it crossed the Mississippi, moving back into Illinois in April 1832: about 1,000 to 1,500 people. Along with discontented Sauks and Meskwakies, it included some 200 Kickapoos who had recently lost their village as well as some followers of the Prophet Wabokieshiek. If contemporary estimates were accurate, it included about 500 warriors as well as women and children. A council of mostly young and inexperienced men plus Black Hawk and the Prophet provided the leadership. As they traveled northeast up the Rock River, they hoped that the nearby tribes would offer support and land for a new village, but few of the other villagers wanted to risk walking into a war. When Black Hawk realized that the hoped-for help was an illusion, he decided to move back to Iowa. Instead, an Illinois militia unit found his camp and attacked. At Stillman's Run the defenders defeated and scattered the volunteers, beginning an unexpected war.[38]

When the fighting began, General Henry Atkinson, then commanding the troops at Jefferson Barracks south of St. Louis, was shuttling troops between Prairie du Chien and Fort Armstrong at Rock Island. Thinking that he needed to prevent a war between the Sioux and Menominees on one side and the Sauks and Meskwakies on the other, he was caught unprepared by the British Band's "invasion" of Illinois. Fearing that the Indians expected to start a war, which was highly unlikely because they had all of the women and children with them, the general called on the governor, John Reynolds, to mobilize the militia, which he did in April. Black Hawk's followers moved up the Rock River, while the band leaders asked Ho-Chunk and Potawatomi chiefs for support. When they declined to help. Black Hawk realized that the British Band stood alone. At that point he decided that "if the White Beaver [Atkinson] came after us, we would go back—as it was useless to think of stopping or going on without provisions."[39]

The members of the British Band never had a chance to retrace their steps down the Rock River, because General Atkinson had allowed the Illinois militiamen to scout for the Indians without any army oversight. When they learned that the Indians were only twenty-five miles away, the governor ordered two battalions of militiamen under Major Isaiah Stillman to find them. On May 14, 1832, when the Indians learned of the white force, Black Hawk claims that he sent men with a white flag to negotiate. Without any interpreter the nervous volunteers fired at the emissaries, charged the Indian camp, and rode into an ambush. The Sauks charged the militiamen: their sudden attack terrified the volunteers, who scattered and fled.[40] This one-sided battle at Stillman's Run ended any hope that the British Band would be allowed to return peacefully to Iowa. Illinois politicians, the militiamen, and Atkinson's force of regulars all sought to catch them and end the conflict.

Seeing the attack by Stillman's force on the flagbearers as white deception, the British Band leaders sent their men out to raid frontier settlements. At the same time American leaders from the president on down demanded a military victory to assure that nearby tribes would stay at peace. This left the Indians moving slowly north into Wisconsin, as they searched for enough food to keep themselves alive. Meanwhile the militiamen returned home, as the regulars failed to locate the British Band. By June 1832 General Atkinson's Army of the Frontier included 629 regular army troops and another 3,196 newly activated Illinois volunteers.[41]

The mounted militia units moved faster than the army infantrymen and eventually found the trail of the retreating starving Indians. Dead horses, scattered camp goods, and an occasional Indian corpse marked the British Band's retreat as it headed west toward the Mississippi. On July 21 the militiamen caught up to the fugitives as they tried to cross the Wisconsin River. They attacked the vastly outnumbered Indians, but Black Hawk's small rear guard held off the whites long enough for the Indians to escape across the river.[42] After the fighting ended, one of the Indian leaders shouted to the attackers that they only wanted to return west and would not fight any longer, but, as at Stillman's Run, the whites had no translator.[43]

After that attack the British Band began to disintegrate. Individual Indians and small families in canoes fled down the Wisconsin River toward the Mississippi, hoping to escape into Iowa, but troops from Fort Crawford at Prairie du Chien patrolled the river and captured many of them. At this point Menominee and Ho-Chunk allies also patrolled the river, capturing canoes loaded with women and children and killing the few men with them.[44] Dakota Sioux warriors, alerted by the whites, moved north from Prairie du Chien to help intercept the fleeing British Band survivors too. As the fugitives got to the Mississippi, the steamboat *Warrior* sailed into view, and the Sauks raised another white flag trying to surrender. Again, as in earlier circumstances, the boat crew had no translator. The whites feared that the white flag was just another ruse, so they opened fire with an artillery piece and killed twenty-three of the fleeing Indians. When the steamer turned south to refuel, Sauk and Meskwakie women tried to escape across the river to Iowa, but some drowned.[45]

By August 1, when the steamboat attacked the fleeing Indians, they were exhausted, many nearly starving, and desperate to escape the pursuing troops and their Menominee and Ho-Chunk allies. The tribal fighters considered the Sauks and Meskwakies to be traditional enemies and proved to be at least as eager to kill the fugitives as Atkinson's troops were. At sunup the regulars and militiamen swarmed down the hills along the Mississippi, trapping the British Band survivors between them and the *Warrior*, which had returned to the battle site. By this time only about 150 Sauk and Meskwakie men remained to defend their families. While they fought, desperate women and children swam to nearby islands, only to be shot by the crew and Menominee men on board. Some of the women carried little children in blankets as they tried to get across the river. Others tried to remain under water with only their noses above the surface, but the attacking Indians shot them too. The victorious attackers killed over 260 of the British Band that day.[46]

Atkinson's troops suffered only modest losses: only 14 of his men died that day. The troops needlessly shot nearly all of the men and boys in the battle itself, while killing or wounding many of the women and children too. Some of the volunteers killed women and children as they tried to flee during the melee. Others joined their Indian allies taking scalps off the dead as they had done earlier after the Battle of Wisconsin Heights less than two weeks earlier. Just as militiamen had done after the Battle of Horseshoe Bend in 1814, the Illinois volunteers committed atrocities, mutilating the Indian corpses. The Battle of Bad Axe ended military operations in the Black War and accomplished its goal of persuading the other tribes of the upper Mississippi Valley to remain at peace for the next generation.

Ash Hollow, 1855

The 1855 battle at Ash Hollow on Blue Water Creek in Nebraska offers a new component in the narrative of U.S. destruction of indigenous people. It occurred as part of a campaign to retaliate and punish Sioux villagers for the 1854 Grattan Massacre at Fort Laramie on the Overland Trail in Wyoming and the violence that followed later that summer. The first massacre in this study to have been carried out entirely by U.S. Army regular troops, it included no Indian allies who helped the whites destroy their traditional enemies or any of the often ill-disciplined volunteers who manned state militia units. Both those two groups tended to kill indiscriminately or to commit atrocities when not supervised closely, but the regulars did not. In fact, once the shooting ended, they located and tended to the wounded Sioux women and children while treating the wounded soldiers. Despite the humane treatment of the prisoners, this devastating attack on the unprepared villagers signaled American willingness to use total-war tactics against the Indians. It gave the much-criticized army leaders a clear example of how to defeat their illusive foes.

The incident began on September 2, 1855. General William S. Harney halted his troops along the North Platte River within sight of the forty-one lodges in Chief Little Thunder's Brulé Sioux camp. According to one of the officers, the Indians seemed unafraid of the soldiers. In fact, he reported that a local trader had brought a message from the camp to

Harney that "if he wanted peace he could have it, or if he wanted war . . . he could have" it.[1] That seems unlikely, because Chief Little Thunder ignored the usual Sioux practice of making sure to get the women and children out of danger and Harney never mentioned getting the message in his reports. Whatever the trader told him, the irascible and profane general responded: "By God, I'm for battle, no peace."[2]

Late that evening Harney met his unit commanders to prepare for battle the next morning. He ordered the troops to move north across the Platte quickly in what became a "most disagreeable night duty." Just after 2 A.M. on September 3, 1855, Colonel Philip St. George Cooke led the mounted dragoons around the Sioux camp to a position behind it to cut off any escape when the attack began. Several hours later Harney ordered the infantry companies to advance toward the village. When they saw the ranks of soldiers marching toward them, the Indians realized the danger. Chief Little Thunder hurried to meet Harney. He said that his people wanted peace, but the general reminded him of the Grattan fight, the mail coach robbery, and repeated raids on immigrants along the overland trail and demanded that the chief turn over the people guilty of those acts. Knowing that the Indian leader would not be "able to deliver up all the butchers of our people, however willing he might have been," Harney continued the advance.[3] In one last desperate effort to keep peace, the chief and other camp leaders rode back carrying an old umbrella, which the soldiers thought was a white flag; but the general was through talking.

The fighting that followed was no real battle. The Indians had not expected an attack or they would have removed the women and children from the camp. As soon as Little Thunder returned to the camp, Harney ordered the infantrymen to advance and begin firing. The unprepared villagers struck their tents hurriedly, leaving their meals still cooking on the campfires. Abandoning most of their equipment and food stores, they fled up the valley. The oncoming soldiers, armed with the newly improved rifles that their commander had located for the expedition, began shooting with deadly effect. Having mostly only bows and arrows or old muskets with a short range, the village defenders could do little to slow their attackers. The overmatched warriors fled from the village to the nearby bluffs and hid in small recesses there. From there the defenders fought back effectively, particularly from one of the larger caves that the soldiers called Hudson's Hole. Sioux resistance from that location brought heavy fire down into the cave from soldiers on a ledge above the cave entrance. They stopped shooting only after the officers heard a crying baby in the cave. When the troops entered it later, they found a dozen dead men and many women and children either dead or wounded.[4]

As soon as Colonel Cooke heard the infantrymen firing from his position behind the Indian camp, he sent his cavalrymen charging into the main body of Sioux as they retreated toward him. His tactic caught the warriors between his men and the foot soldiers and blocked their escape. The move worked, except that one troop of the dragoons missed a gap in the assault and some of the warriors raced away. One observer reported that as the Indians fled "we poured a plunging fire upon them . . . knocking them out of their saddles, right and left."[5] As they rode past the soldiers, the fleeing Indians stopped repeatedly to pick up wounded or dead comrades. A captive later said that during the battle she had seen "soldiers galloping after groups of old men, women, and children who were running for their lives."[6] While the dragoons pursued the fugitives "for five or six miles over rugged country," they "killed a large number of them and completely dispers[ed] the whole party," a pleased Harney reported.[7]

The fighting at the camp lasted only half an hour, but it took much of the day for the dragoons pursuing the fleeing Sioux to get back to the camp. There the triumphant general reported that his men had taken nearly seventy prisoners, all women and children, and killed eighty-six fighters while wounding five more. His losses included four dead, four wounded, and one man missing. The number for Indian casualties likely underestimated the slaughter, because it overlooked the wounded who died in flight and the bodies of their dead comrades that the fleeing warriors had carried away during their escape. Whatever the total number of casualties was, battlefield accounts suggested that nearly half of the villagers had been killed or wounded. Lieutenant G. K. Warren noted the sounds of "wounded women and children crying and moaning, horribly mangled by the bullets."[8] While the army medical officers treated the wounded captives, the victorious soldiers left the Indian corpses for the scavengers.

This reflected Harney's attitude. He ignored the slaughter of the women and children and certainly expressed no remorse for any atrocities. Instead he boasted that "the result was what I anticipated and hoped for." The Indians "were retaliated upon fully for their hostile acts towards our people." He defended the attack because soldiers found military items taken from Grattan's men, the scalps of two white women, and letters taken from the November mail robbery in the deserted lodges. Later he explained his attack on the village to Little Thunder, saying that he told the chief, "Yours was the first band of Sioux I met when I came to fight, but if I had met any other band it would have been the same."[9]

This incident opened the so-called First Sioux War on the plains. Although the Indian groups living there in the 1840s fought continuing wars against each other, they usually avoided trouble with the increasing numbers of pioneers traveling through their home territories. The development of the Oregon, California, and Mormon Trails across the central plains and the gold rush that followed brought thousands of Americans onto and through an area that the tribes considered their homeland. To protect the people moving west in 1848, the army established Fort Kearny, on the south side of the Platte River in central Nebraska. A year later it added Fort Laramie farther west in Wyoming to its list of tiny isolated outposts on the plains. Designed to keep peace between the Indians and the invading whites, these small garrisons of infantrymen proved almost totally ineffective.

Despite the new outposts, by 1849 Indian office officers had begun to worry that the massive numbers of whites traveling west would antagonize the Plains tribes and that they would turn their fighting men against the migrants. They asked Congress for authorization and funds to negotiate peace treaties with the major tribes of the region but, the legislators were too busy hammering out the Compromise of 1850 in their continuing attempt to settle the ever more bitter debate about extending slavery into the West.[10] That agreement created two new territories, Utah and New Mexico, which added to the pressures on the Plains tribes by encouraging more Americans to move west.

Assuming that it had settled the slavery issue Congress turned its attention to Indian Affairs and passed funds for negotiating a treaty to assure safety for Americans moving west. That appropriation led to the appointment of former mountain man Thomas Fitzpatrick and David Mitchell, superintendent of Indian Affairs at St. Louis, as commissioners to sign agreements with Plains tribes living north of the Arkansas River and west of the Missouri. They invited all the major tribes from the region, and some ten thousand Indians from eight of them gathered for the council to be held at Fort Laramie. Three other tribes, the Comanches, Kiowas, and Kiowa Apaches, boycotted the meeting because it was in territory belonging to their Sioux enemies.

So many Indians attended the ceremonies that the commissioners had to shift the location about thirty miles downstream to Horse Creek, the term that most tribes used later to describe the treaty. Many of the chiefs knew and trusted Fitzpatrick, and each group described the boundaries of their land to him. When the Sioux claimed the Black Hills in South Dakota as theirs, the Cheyennes and Arapahos objected heatedly. Years later an Arapaho chief complained that the region was "part Sioux, and part mine," but now "they claim all this land."[11]

Despite what the commissioners saw as minor disagreements between tribes over their land, on September 17, 1851, the American negotiators concluded what became the Treaty of Fort Laramie. It promised the Indians that the United States would pay them $50,000 a year for the next fifty years as compensation for damage to their land that white pioneers might cause.[12] The negotiators hoped that the annual payments of food and supplies would help keep the villagers from raiding the settlers streaming west through their country. Superintendent Mitchell justified the half-century of payments by saying that he expected it would take that long for the Plains tribes to become sedentary. Given the social organization within the tribes, which allowed individuals almost total personal freedom to raid or fight, the chiefs' marks on the papers failed to prevent future violence. Further complicating matters, Congress, in its wisdom, reduced the payments from fifty to only fifteen years, reducing the critically needed subsistence promised in the treaty.[13]

The 1851 Treaty of Fort Laramie or Horse Creek illustrated the gulf separating American and Indian desires and realities. According to the 1831 *Cherokee v. Georgia* ruling by the Supreme Court, Indian tribes were considered to be "domestic dependent nations."[14] This meant that each tribe had to be considered a unified group rather than a mere collection of villages, clans, and bands that usually operated independently. Therefore, in order to negotiate agreements U.S. officials needed to have a head chief for each tribe. Repeatedly they tried to persuade each group to recognize one chief so that officials could pressure him to get his followers to obey the treaty. That also gave the bureaucrats and military commanders someone to blame when violence occurred. Regardless of how many times tribal leaders objected that their people did not recognize and would not obey head chiefs, Americans refused to accept that idea. To them that argument only allowed the chiefs to ignore their duties and refuse to cooperate. American refusal to recognize and accept indigenous social and political reality explains much of the apparent confusion about how best to deal with the Indians on the plains.[15]

Although the Indians objected to the hordes of pioneers streaming through their home territories, they usually stayed away from the overland trails. The treaty kept peace for a time between Indians and whites but not among the contending tribes.[16] That changed three years later during a late summer 1854 incident near Fort Laramie. Some 4,800 Oglalas, Brulés, and Miniconjous had come to fort expecting to get their promised treaty rations. As often happened, the officials responsible for delivering the food and other presents were late. Waiting for several weeks, the large encampment exhausted the nearby grass, water, and game. While the hungry Indians waited for the promised food, a wagon train of Scandinavian Mormons going west to Salt Lake City passed their camps. It is not entirely clear what happened, but one of the immigrants' cows ran into the Brulé camp. High Forehead, one of the Sioux, killed the animal. The hungry villagers quickly roasted it and ate it. The immigrants continued to Fort Laramie, where the owner of the cow complained to Lieutenant Hugh Fleming, then in command. He sent for Chief Conquering Bear, the man recognized as Lakota head chief in the 1851 treaty. The chief knew that the villagers had to pay the owner for his cow and offered the man a horse. The local trader James Bordeaux offered him $10, but he demanded $25. At that point one of the men suggested giving him a cow from the herd on its way to the fort as part of the treaty, but the owner refused all efforts to settle the dispute.[17]

Even though responsibility for settling disputes of this kind belonged to the civilian Indian agent expected to arrive in a few days, Lieutenant Fleming intervened. He demanded that Conquering Bear bring High Forehead to the fort. The chief told him that he had no power to force the man to surrender because he was a Miniconjou and only a guest at the Brulé village. When the lieutenant insisted that the chief force High Forehead to surrender, he refused and told Fleming that he should go to the camp and arrest him. Angrily the officer told him to expect a detail of troops to do that the next day, although he had orders to let the civilian officials deal with such disputes. When Conquering Bear told the other chiefs what had happened, they held a council to try to avoid any violence. At the same time, however, many of the younger men began preparing for a fight.[18] Their opposing actions show why peace on the frontier remained fragile.

The chiefs' council decided to send Man-Afraid-of-His-Horses to the fort the next morning to calm the situation. But by the time he got there Fleming had decided to send his subordinate, acting second lieutenant John Grattan, newly graduated from West Point, to arrest High Forehead. As the soldiers got their equipment in order, Man-Afraid-of-His-Horses talked to both Lieutenant Fleming and Grattan. He told Grattan, "You had better not go . . . there are a great many Sioux," but the inexperienced young officer ignored his advice.[19] Grattan led a party of twenty-nine men, including an interpreter and equipped with two small howitzers and an army wagon, confidently out of the fort. Excited with his first independent command and determined to succeed, at 3:00 P.M. Grattan ordered his men to begin their eight-mile march to the Brulé village.

From the start the interpreter, Auguste Lucien, proved reluctant to follow Grattan into the Sioux villages. Drinking heavily, he proved a major liability when the troops neared the Sioux lodges. Man-Afraid-of-His-Horses reported that he tried to dissuade Grattan a second time, telling him that "there a heap of lodges" ahead. The lieutenant replied, "That is good, as I am going to war on them."[20] About halfway to the Lakota camps, the soldiers stopped at Gratiot's American Fur Company trading post. Men there warned the brash lieutenant about the danger ahead. He ignored their advice and continued the march.

When they neared the encampments, Grattan had the men deploy the two artillery pieces, only then learning that few of them had any experience with the weapons. Seeing the soldiers approach, the Sioux prepared to defend themselves, drove their horse herds into camp, and rode out to surround the troops. By now the interpreter was roaring drunk and rode around taunting the Sioux by shouting that "we have come to wipe you out."[21]

Despite the nearby traders' pleas to Grattan to remain peaceful, one of the soldiers opened fire. Mounted Sioux men overran and killed all but one of the members of the detachment, who died a few days later.

Conquering Bear, who had tried to avoid the violence, was one of the first Indians that the troops killed. Auguste, the drunken interpreter who had caused so much tension that afternoon, died, riddled by many Sioux arrows. As their chief Conquering Bear lay dying, many of the young men wanted revenge. Some talked of attacking Fort Laramie. Fortunately for the garrison, which now included fewer than twenty men, tribal leaders persuaded them to avoid the fort. Instead they looted the supplies meant for them stored at James Bordeau's trading post and the nearby American Fur Company post too. Having taken the long-awaited food and trade items, most of the Sioux bands moved away from the Platte and the immigrant trails.[22]

On the spot investigations by the army and Indian officials produced contradictory results. Indian agent John Whitfield criticized both the lieutenants at the fort. He blamed Hugh Fleming for causing the "catastrophe" by trying to arrest High Head for having killed the immigrant's cow. According to the agent, if the officer had obeyed the law the Indians would have paid the Mormon for his cow, which they had offered to do. Whitfield also blamed Lieutenant Grattan for not having another interpreter when he realized that Auguste was drunk and that his insults were enraging the Sioux. The agent went on to question Grattan's judgment in leading such a small and hostile force up to the Indian camp and his unwillingness to listen to both Indian and white advice about the danger of his actions. He rejected claims that the Indians had lured Grattan's force into their camp to kill them, because they always avoid war when the women and children were present and had remained peaceful despite acts of minor theft along the trail.[23]

As one might expect, Major Oscar Winship, then on an inspection tour of frontier forts, concluded differently. He accepted Lieutenant Fleming's report, which tried to blame Chief Conquering Bear because he had refused to hand over High Head to the soldiers. The major submitted his report on the incident without interviewing any of the Sioux. Although he admitted that it was "impossible to ascertain which party struck the first blow," he concluded that the Indians had started the shooting. When the trader and close spectator James Bordeau testified that the soldiers had started the fight, the major rejected his statement because he was married to a Sioux woman and therefore was not a credible witness. Clearly Winship chose to deflect any blame for the disaster away from the army, already in a bad light because of having lost most of the garrison at Fort Laramie and having killed only one Indian, Chief Conquering Bear. Instead of condemning Grattan's blameworthy arrogance and stupidity, he ignored the negative evidence and called for a campaign against the Sioux. "Clearly the time has now fully arrived," he wrote, "for teaching these barbarians a lesson to appreciate and respect the power, the justice, the generosity and magnanimity of the United States."[24]

The Franklin Pierce administration accepted the military's version of the event, as did many eastern newspapers. The president and secretary of war Jefferson Davis claimed that the Sioux had provoked the attack to have an excuse to raid the nearby warehouses. That seems a flimsy motivation when the food was theirs to begin with and they would have had it in a few days when the agent arrived. The press issued a series of highly incendiary articles all blaming the Sioux. One New York city paper labeled the incident a massacre, while another demanded a campaign to punish the indigenous people for the "Indian outrages" they had committed. Western papers joined the chorus: one discussed the "treacherous slaughter of United States troops." In St. Louis the *Daily Missouri Republican* claimed that Conquering Bear had killed Lieutenant Grattan with a lance before the battle began. An Oregon paper reported an entirely fictitious story describing how a Sioux and Cheyenne attack on a 300-person wagon train left only nineteen survivors. These sentiments encouraged the president, the secretary of war, and army Commanding General Winfield Scott to conclude that they should organize an expedition to punish the Sioux.[25]

Almost immediately after destroying Grattan's force, Sioux leaders met to decide what actions they needed to take. During late August they held debates between those calling for war to retaliate for the whites' unprovoked attack and those who urged caution. Young men eager for a fight asked their traders and agents for guns and ammunition, made new arrows, and gathered more horses. Their easy victory over the soldiers persuaded some groups that they could do without the promised annuity food and other goods. Reports from the frontier noted that the Hunkpapas and Blackfeet had told their agent that they could live without the white goods, and the Yanktons did the same. Still, the need to gather food for winter and the buffalo robes needed to pay their traders kept most men busy and off the warpath that fall.[26]

As the army began its plans for an expedition into Sioux country, new reports of violence and danger continued to arrive. On November 13, 1854, a small group of Sioux raiders stopped the U.S. Mail party headed from Salt Lake City to Fort Laramie, killing three men, wounding another, and making off with $10,000 worth of gold. Some observers feared that this was an effort to stop travel on the overland trails, but that never occurred. Instead travelers coming east from California reported that the Indians told them that "they would not molest immigrants but intended to kill every U.S. officer or soldier they met."[27] Except for some minor thievery they ignored the overland travelers.

Even before hearing these reports, Jefferson Davis had decided to authorize a major expedition against the Sioux and had chosen a friend to lead it for the task: Colonel and Brevet Brigadier General William S. Harney. Commander of the Second Dragoons, Harney was an experienced career officer with broad experience, having served in the Missouri Valley, the Black Hawk War, the Second Seminole War, and the war with Mexico as well as on the plains. A big, impressive-looking man with a dangerous temper and foul vocabulary to match, he began his new command with energy and competence. Determined to end the mounted Indians' raiding, Secretary Davis called for taking a hard line by using total war tactics against the hostile groups. Other than a vague outline calling for a campaign that would "strike an effective blow" against hostile groups, Davis and General Scott gave few instructions except to call for Harney to begin "as early in the season as may be found practicable."[28]

Harney agreed with the secretary of war that to halt attacks on the overland trails "the savages must be crushed."[29] To carry out the first major army campaign against the Sioux since the war with Mexico had ended, the general needed to gather troops from units scattered from Texas to Carlisle Barracks in Pennsylvania. When assembled in late summer 1855, his force included units from the Second, Sixth, and Tenth Infantry; the Fourth Artillery; and his unit, the Second Dragoons. Totaling some 600 men, his command was far smaller than those in either the earlier Red Stick War or Black Hawk War. Unlike those two conflicts, these troops included only U.S. Army regulars. They had no Indian guides or auxiliaries or civilian militia men, so the resulting atrocities all came directly from the soldiers' actions. As he waited for the scattered units to arrive, Harney worked to gather the weapons, horses, and supplies needed for the campaign. In early June he ordered several companies of the mounted dragoons to patrol the immigrant trails between Forts Kearny and Laramie. As they rode along the Platte River, they passed several Sioux camps near the river without incident.[30]

While Harney struggled to gather and move troops in preparation for the campaign, he faced continual opposition from officials in the Office of Indian Affairs. Beginning in 1849, when oversight of Indian Affairs shifted to the newly created Interior Department, fierce debates between the civilian and military led to confused and contradictory actions toward the Indians. George Manypenny, the commissioner of Indian Affairs, opposed the expedition to punish the Sioux openly. Along with his subordinates he blamed the ill-advised actions of Lieutenants Fleming and Grattan for the death of Chief Conquering Bear and the destruction of Grattan's command the year before. At this point Manypenny announced the appointment of a new Sioux agent, Thomas S. Twiss, a former army officer. After a brief inspection Twiss announced that the Oglalas and Brulés were peaceful and encouraged them to move south of the Platte. He wrote that the Sioux posed no threat to whites in the area and that the "difficulties [with the Indians] have been magnified by false and malicious reports." As far as he could tell, "there is not . . . a single hostile Indian."[31]

Following the agent's advice, many of the Oglalas and Brulés moved their camps south of the Platte to avoid being attacked and to show that they were at peace. A few of the villages ignored Twiss and remained north of the river, even when their trader James Bordeau sent messengers urging them to do what the agent said. Chief Little Thunder, who succeeded Conquering Bear as leader, chose to remain at his campsite because the hunters had killed many buffalo and they had a large amount of meat to dry for their winter food supply and hides to cure as well. Apparently the village leaders assumed that they were not at war with the United States, although some members of his band had tried to raid the Pawnee and Omaha tribes. His people had not attacked overland trail companies, and after the capture of the Salt Lake mail coach Little Thunder had tried to return the surviving mules. They had watched as dragoons patrolled the overland trails without bothering the Brulés camped at Ash Hollow between Forts Kearny and Laramie just north of the Platte. Confident in their own strength and having seen no reason to post guards, the villagers took no defensive actions as the troops marched into the vicinity.[32]

Despite being unable to get the rest of the dragoon company from Texas, and the arrival of the companies of the Fourth Artillery without any usable weapons, Harney's superiors urged him to continue the expedition. On July 5 new orders directed him to ignore the lateness of the season, move west, and "strike a blow" against the Indians. However, when he tried to follow army practice and hire Indian guides. The Indians declined, having been told by their agents that they might lose their annuities if they guided the troops. After many delays, his 600-man force marched out of Fort Leavenworth on August 4, 1885, and along the Platte to Fort Kearny. As they moved west news of continuing Indian raids and rumors of Sioux hostility poured in, only making the general more determined to punish them. Just over two weeks later the column reached Fort Kearny.[33]

On August 24 Harney led the troops out of Fort Kearny, heading northwest along the overland trail toward Fort Laramie. They marched westward for ten days covering about 180 miles and came to Ash Hollow, the reputed location of hostile Sioux. Little Thunder's village with forty-one lodges stood only six miles up the Blue Water Creek from the Platte. They knew of the soldiers' movements but apparently saw nothing to fear from their presence.

Harney's destructive attack on Little Thunder's village had frightened some of the Sioux while angering others. His next move, marching the command northeast from the Platte River to Fort Pierre in South Dakota, proved that the army could penetrate the very heart of tribal territory. Sioux band leaders were persuaded that to have peace they needed to meet with "Mad Bear," as they called the general. They surrendered the men who had robbed the mail stage in November 1854 and returned many of the animals stolen from Fort Laramie earlier. At Fort Pierre Miniconjou leaders surrendered more stolen horses. Jefferson Davis encouraged Harney to hold a council to negotiate peace. In May 1856 some five thousand Indians arrived for the council. The general demanded that they end attacks along the overland trail, stop raiding nearby tribes, return stolen government property and animals, and surrender High Head, the man who had stolen the Mormon's cow at Fort Laramie, setting off the Grattan Massacre. He promised to release the prisoners taken at Blue Water Creek and told them that the government would restore their annuities.[34]

This campaign and later peace negotiations demonstrated that the Indians could not depend on their isolation as a defense. Before Harney's operation the army had been content to station small numbers of infantrymen at a few small, scattered posts. Because of their size and lack of mobility, these troops had little impact on the Indians' village life or practice, but this new tactic brought a well-coordinated force deep into their homeland. The fight at Ash Hollow offered military planners their first successful example of total war against the Indians. Military planners avoided the tactic, particularly its use during the winter, until after the Civil War, when it became standard practice. Army attacks on villages raised the number of civilian casualties in the later campaigns and increased public criticism of military barbarity but eventually pacified the West.

CHAPTER 4

Bear River, 1863

When the American Civil War began in 1861, it had a major effect on the nation's dealings with the western Indians. The demand for troops to replace those killed in the increasingly bitter fighting in the East persuaded the War Department to move regular army units there. In Texas and a few other places the army closed small isolated posts; in others it just withdrew most of the units. By 1862 the War Department and the states had created new divisions of volunteers to replace the regulars who had left the West. Frequently former pioneers, these soldiers carried existing anti-Indian views into their dealings with the western tribes. Many of them had long experience with horses, livestock, firearms, and the harsh environment, making them more effective than the regular forces' mix of immigrants and often unemployed city dwellers. Because some career officers received appointments several ranks higher in the volunteers than had they stayed in the regulars, a few western units benefited from having experienced and ambitious leaders. Those were the exceptions: in most cases local business and political leaders with varied military experience headed the new volunteer regiments. During the war, some of these units fought effectively, and others brutally, in their campaigns against the western Indians.[1] During their service they committed two of the most horrendous Indian massacres in American history, at Bear River in 1863 and at Sand Creek a year later.

While the new volunteer units increased the number of troops in the West to 15,000 men, the continuing flood of pioneers moving into or through Indian country kept tensions high.[2] Gold and silver discoveries in Colorado, Nevada, Montana, and the Northwest lured thousands of miners into those areas and led the government to establish new territories or states quickly there. Pioneer farmers joined the miners as they moved west on the Overland Trail from Salt Lake City. Thousands of Mormons helped to fill many uninhabited areas with white farms and towns as they fled persecution. These developments during the war persuaded the Abraham Lincoln administration that to retain the westerners' support for the union it had to keep mail and telegraph services functioning and protect the settlers. To do that, it justified stationing many of the volunteers in the West. Yet the troops could not be everywhere, and their mere presence did little to deter interracial incidents between traveling pioneers and the indigenous groups whose country the whites passed through.

This became an issue during the early 1860s for the Shoshonis and their neighbors as many whites crossed through northwestern Utah and southern Idaho. There Shoshonis and Bannocks objected to the seeming endless groups of wagon trains carrying immigrants west, all taking their game and other resources. Without any way to replace the animals, roots, seeds, and grasses that the intruding Americans took or destroyed, indigenous leaders tried to get livestock or other food from the immigrants. As a result, the intruding whites accused the Indians of being beggars and thieves, while the tribal people complained that the migrants ruined their land and mistreated them. In this situation the whites fought with the Indians and asked federal officials to punish or remove them.

That situation prompted Colonel Patrick Connor to lead his unit of California Volunteers in an attack on a Shoshoni village on Bear River in southeastern Idaho. Connor, a poor Irish immigrant, had begun his military service in 1839 as a private, enlisting in the First Dragoons. After serving his five-year term, he left the army, but in 1846 he joined the Texas Volunteers and his unit elected him a first lieutenant. After being wounded at the Battle of Buena Vista, he resigned and remained a civilian until 1862, when he gained an appointment as colonel of the Third California Volunteers and was ordered to lead his unit to northern Utah. Apparently an effective leader, he faced two challenges once there. First he had to deal with Brigham Young and the Mormons occupying the area, and second he had to protect immigrants on the Oregon Trail from attack by the Shoshoni people living near it.[3]

Connor's experiences mirrored those of other frontier commanders. He received frequent reports of Indian depredations and complaints that his force failed to protect overland immigrants effectively. When he did act, the action resembled many of the other incidents in this book. It began as combat and, in the heat of battle, degenerated into a massacre. While his after-battle report says nothing about atrocities, enough other firsthand accounts describe them in detail to remove any doubt that they occurred. Overlooking the atrocities seems out of character for Connor: earlier when ordering a subordinate to "destroy every male Indian whom you may encounter," he went on to caution that "in no instance will you molest women and children."[4] Clearly, when the shooting stopped, he and the other officers focused on getting medical attention for their wounded men and gathering the dead soldiers' bodies rather than supervising the way the enlisted men acted at the scene. As a result the after-the-battle savagery at Bear River, which included killing the wounded and widespread raping of female prisoners, marked it as one of the most brutal Indian-white encounters in American western history.

Connor's almost total destruction of Shoshoni Chief Bear Hunter's camp resembled General Harney's savage 1855 attack on Sioux Chief Little Thunder's village in Nebraska. Like Harney's message to the Sioux that the troops would punish them, Connor's action warned other Shoshoni bands that the troops would retaliate against them for more attacks on immigrant trains on the Oregon Trail. While some local whites praised Connor's victory, his troops' actions after the fighting ended led to harsh criticism within a generation. Historian Hubert Howe Bancroft pointed out that "had the savages [Indians] committed this deed, it would pass into history as a butchery, or massacre." More recently, Mae Parry, a descendant of Little Thunder's band, harshly attacked Connor's actions. She described his preemptive strike: "without so much as asking the Indians for the guilty party, the Colonel and his men began to fire on the Indians. . . . No butcher could have murdered any better than Colonel Connor and his vicious California volunteers."[5] This seems like a fair assessment of what happened.

To be sure, earlier Shoshoni actions played a central role leading up to this event. These people lived in several distinct bands in northwestern Utah, eastern Nevada, and southern Idaho. Some of the northwestern Shoshonis had occupied the Cache Valley area for generations. Each year they collected seeds, berries, and nuts, dug roots and bulbs, gathered fish and waterfowl, hunted game varying from ground squirrels and wood-chucks to elk and buffalo, and visited the local hot springs.[6] For genera-tions the remoteness of their homeland limited contacts with whites except for the mountain men who trapped in or crossed through the area. During the 1840s, that changed dramatically as pioneers traveling west on the Oregon and California Trails disrupted some of their move-ments and depleted their local resources.

Yet at first the increasing number of immigrants in their country appears not to have angered most of the Indians. Many travelers' accounts described meeting small Indian bands, which fed them and traded with-out any violence. Other whites feared the indigenous people and reported their actions as hostile. No matter what worried travelers said, Indian thefts of animals for food occurred much more often than did dangerous attacks on immigrant trains. The most exhaustive study of white-Indian relations on the Overland Trail concludes that the travelers' fears of Indian violence proved overblown and that the intruders killed more Indians than the Indians killed whites traveling west.[7]

The situation changed in the 1840s, when Mormon pioneers arrived. Unlike the other whites, they were not just immigrants headed farther west but permanent settlers who intended to stay. Minor incidents with the Indians prompted Brigham Young to advocate a policy that it was "cheaper to feed them than to fight them."[8] Although he urged the new settlers to keep peace, the increasing numbers of white farmers drastically strained Shoshoni resources. As the newcomers cleared land and planted crops, they killed or frightened much-needed game from the area, often leaving the Indians without their traditional food sources. The Indians com-plained that they, not the invading Mormons, owned the land and wanted the whites to pay them for its use. Church leaders and pioneers alike rejected that idea. They denied the tribal claim by saying that "the land belongs to our father in heaven, and we calculate to plow and plant it." This left the hungry indigenous villagers few options, and some of them began to levy rent by "taking a share of the grain for the use of the land."[9]

During their first few years of contacts, the two groups usually traded amicably. The peace remained fragile, however, and a few whites killed Indians in several violent incidents. In one instance a settler found an Indian taking ears of corn from his garden. After ordering the man to leave, he shot and killed him for not walking away quickly enough. In another instance pursuing Mormons shot one of a small party of Shoshonis who stole some horses from one of the new settlements. Yet, despite the scattered thievery and turbulence, interracial dealings remained mostly peaceful. Indians even helped the settlers to celebrate holidays by marching in several local parades.[10] However, Brigham Young's effort to encourage new Mormon settlements in the Cache Valley put so much pressure on the villagers' food supply that some of the Indian bands faced gradual starvation.

That led to increasing depredations when Indian men saw the Mormons' cattle and draft animals as good replacements for the native game that the intruders had driven away. Racist immigrants beat or murdered Indians that they met along the trail. For example, when an Indian man visiting an immigrant camp caused the guide's horse to rear and nearly throw his rider to the ground, the guide's son shot the visitor. In another case, after members of a wagon train raped and murdered some Snake women, their families retaliated against later immigrants. In 1851 some whites drove Indians away from one of their favorite camping sites at gunpoint. Not surprisingly, the villagers attacked the group the next day.[11] After encountering raiders the whites often attacked the next Indians they met, without bothering to learn whether they were guilty or innocent or worrying about how the enraged Indians would treat later travelers. Indians stopping to trade occasionally were accused of stealing livestock when the whites' inattention had allowed the animals to stray from the wagon train. At other times, real theft occurred, which infuriated the immigrants. One group of travelers reported: "After that we shot at every Indian we saw—this soon cleared the way."[12]

Throughout the early 1850s the local Indian bands realized that the white immigrants were destroying the wildlife that they depended on as well as depleting the forage available for their horses. So they turned to begging and trying to trade with the wagon trains, but the travelers often treated them badly. This led to frequent misunderstandings, thievery, violent actions, and retaliations that shaped interracial meetings along the trail for the rest of the decade. These incidents gradually escalated and in 1854 led to the Ward Party Massacre. This included the grisly torture and rape of captive women, the torture of their children, and the deaths of twenty white immigrants and an unknown number of Indians.

The six wagons of the Ward party had split off from a larger wagon train as it passed through the Boise Valley near the Snake River. By mid-August of 1854 they had met small groups of Shoshonis. Despite their fear of Indian raids, one of the travelers had provoked them by a thoughtless and cruel act a few weeks earlier: he threw hot ashes on the bare feet of an Indian who got too close to the breakfast he was cooking. The victim of this attack left in a rage.[13]

When the Ward party stopped for lunch on August 20, several Indians hoping to trade for a horse suddenly rushed up and rode off with one. At that point the frightened immigrants hitched their teams and began to leave the camp. As they drove off, more Indians surrounded them, so the pioneers corralled their wagons just as the Shoshonis began shooting. The attackers appear to have been well armed and killed or wounded the men quickly. Then they drove the wagon with the women and children in it off the trail and into the brush.[14]

Rescuers reached the scene two days later, on August 22. They reported locating a burned wagon and the scattered bodies of the dead men. Then they found one of the young women, who had been raped, tortured, and then shot. Nearby they came across the naked corpse of another woman who had been scalped before her head had been smashed to a "perfect jelly." The mutilated body of another victim, Margaret Ward, lay nearby. The charred remains of several children showed that they had been burned alive over a campfire. The searchers reported that they could not find the last three of the children.[15] This attack was the most widely reported serious incident along the trail in Idaho in several years. It illustrated the volatile relations between the intruding whites and the local indigenous groups and led to a gradual increase of U.S. military forces in the region.

For the next several years travelers reported little fighting, but that calm ended in 1859 when Indian raiders attacked four immigrant trains and a force of dragoons patrolling the trail. In June, August, and September of the next year the Shoshonis increased their raids on the travelers. The September 9–10, 1860, Utter Massacre proved to be the most serious. That train included forty-four people traveling in eight wagons with more than a hundred ox-teams, horses, cattle, and dogs. On September 9 the party found the bones of a man killed by the Indians two weeks earlier, along with an account warning of his death written on a nearby board. Soon nearly a hundred Shoshoni or Bannock warriors appeared, painted and chanting what the immigrants assumed to be their war songs. The party hurried to corral the wagons and drove the animals into the protective circle. When the shouting Indians failed to stampede the animals, they approached, claiming to be peaceful but hungry. Hoping to avert an attack, the travelers fed their unwelcome visitors before returning to the trail. That tactic failed: just before noon the Indians came again, this time killing and wounding several of the immigrants and wounding many of the animals. The fighting continued that night and all the next day: Indian shots or arrows killed eleven of the whites.[16]

By this time the terrified immigrants feared that the Indians would kill them all and tried to escape by putting most of their belongings on four of the wagons and leaving the others for their attackers to pillage. They mounted three former soldiers on the best horses, hoping that those men could lead them to the river, and followed in the last four wagons. Late that afternoon, soon after they left, the Indians swarmed around the remaining wagons, cutting holes in the canvas tops and shooting at everyone. When night came on September 10, twenty-two of the pioneers walked away, abandoning some of the wounded and dying. They traveled at night for several days and had so little food that they killed and roasted one of their two dogs. On September 18, exhausted and nearly starving, the fugitives stopped to build a couple of small brush shelters. After several weeks in this camp, people began dying of starvation. The survivors decided to eat their bodies to remain alive. Rescuers reached the haggard survivors nearly six weeks later, in late October.[17] These two devastating attacks on overland immigrants and other raids along the trail led the settlers, travelers, and authorities to call for more troops and stronger punishment of the Indians.

These demands became shriller in September 1862, as reports of new attacks on immigrants trickled in. Responding to a raid that killed twelve travelers, Colonel Patrick Connor, commanding the Third California Volunteers, then located at Salt Lake City, ordered Major Edward McGarry to capture the murderers. If successful, he was to hang them immediately and "leave their bodies exposed as an example of what evil-doers may expect."[18] The major's force failed to locate the attackers but did meet small groups of Shoshonis whom they shot as they were fleeing. One of the companies captured fourteen Indian men and shot most of them when they tried to escape by jumping into the river. Shortly after that the soldiers captured another six men. McGarry released two, demanding that they bring in those who had taken part in the massacre. If they failed to bring the attackers to him the next day, the major threatened that he would kill his four hostages. The next day, as promised, he ordered the prisoners shot and their bodies dumped into the river. On this foray the volunteers killed twenty-four Indian men, none of whom had taken any hostile actions toward the troops. While Colonel Connor praised these actions, McGarry's unprovoked killings infuriated the Shoshonis.[19]

Indian raids and military forays continued in the fall of 1862, when Shoshoni bands killed one group of ten men and attacked other travelers. In response Utah judge John Kinney signed a warrant for the arrest of chiefs Bear Hunter, Sanpitch, and Sagwitch. By this time, and without any civilian prodding, Colonel Connor had decided to lead a winter attack against the Shoshonis. "Being satisfied that they were part of the same band who had been murdering immigrants on the overland mail route for the past fifteen years . . . I determined . . . to chastise them if possible," he wrote.[20] Acting to avoid any chance that the Indians would learn of his intent, on January 21, 1863, a decoy force of sixty-nine infantry men marched away from camp with fifteen wagons loaded with supplies and ammunition and two howitzers. Two days later Connor led 220 cavalrymen along the trail. The two units planned to meet before they reached the Indian village later. By September 28, traveling through bitter cold and snow up to four feet deep, the infantrymen had to abandon the two howitzers well before they reached the battle site.

Connor's mounted force began its frigid march toward the Shoshoni camp at 3:00 A.M. on January 29, 1863. Having joined the infantry three hours later, they crossed the nearly frozen river. Their movement aroused the sleeping villagers as they began the attack on the Indian camp.[21] Chief Bear Hunter's village contained seventy-five lodges and about four hundred people. Apparently the Indians felt secure in their well-protected camp, and the war leader Chief Bear Hunter expected the army officers to demand that they surrender those guilty of local raiding. Instead of negotiating, Colonel Connor had come to fight. Clearly the soldiers' assault that morning caught the Shoshoni leaders by surprise, as they had made no effort to move the women and children out of harm's way.

Prior to leaving Camp Douglas, Connor had ordered every man to carry forty rounds of ammunition for his rifle and another thirty rounds for his pistol, so there was no worry that they might run out of ammunition before the battle ended. Once the soldiers crossed to the Indians' side of Bear River, the colonel sent them around both flanks of the village: they attacked from the front and both sides. A heavy growth of willows obscured the troopers' view and protected the defenders early in the fighting. When the Indians' heavy fire killed and wounded many of the attackers, Connor ordered the troops to charge from all sides. For the next two hours the fighters shot and stabbed each other in heavy man-to-man fighting. At 10:00 that morning, when the combat ended, the victorious troops counted 224 Indian bodies and estimated that another 50 people had died while trying to escape across the river. Connor's force suffered 23 men killed and another 50 wounded. A *San Francisco Bulletin* reporter with the troops wrote that "the carnage . . . in the ravine was horrible. Warrior piled on warrior . . . with here and there a squaw and papoose, who had been accidentally killed."[22]

While contemporary accounts gave differing figures of Indian deaths and casualties, the result was clear. A local resident reported that about 90 women and children had died in the fighting. Connor gave the number of captives as 160. According to the local Indian agent, James D. Doty, "The Indians state that there were 255 men, women, and children killed in the late engagement on Bear River." Observers at the scene reported that when the shooting ended individual soldiers killed all of the seriously wounded Indians by hitting them "in the head with an axe." One soldier shot a baby found in the arms of its dead mother in what he described as an act of "mercy to the babe." A civilian observer stated that "the way the soldiers used the Squaws after the battle was shameful." He reported that often they killed Indian women "because they would not submit quietly to be ravished, and other squaws were ravished in the agony of death." Several days later a local Mormon leader reported that Indians who visited their village "all are familiar with the conduct of the troops toward the Squaws." He continued that the women were afraid to visit the white settlements because they feared that the militiamen might be there and treat them as they had done on the battlefield.[23]

Taking care to treat wounded soldiers and Indians, Connor's force searched through the half-destroyed lodges, gathering combs, mirrors, blankets, cooking utensils, and the covers off immigrant wagons as well as recovering at least 1,000 bushels of wheat, barrels of flour, and meat all clearly taken from whites passing through the area. The victors captured 175 horses as well as Indian buffalo robes, bows and arrows, pipes, and weapons, which they kept as souvenirs. While gathering this battlefield loot, they burned what was left of the lodges and ignored the piles of Indian corpses. Six months later many observers reported that skeletons still littered the site, "their bones scattered by the wolves."[24]

The volunteers won the battle, but they paid a horrific price. When the fighting ended, twenty-two enlisted men and one officer had died of their wounds. Apparently the Indian fighters had become good marksmen: many of the wounded and killed suffered wounds to the body where they would do the most harm. Marching and riding through the bitter cold also took a major toll. Nearly eighty of the volunteers could not take part in the attack because they had frozen their feet before reaching Bear Hunter's camp. Nearly a month later Connor reported that ninety men were still sick, another twenty-two in the hospital, and several others had lost fingers or toes because of frostbite.[25] Despite the hardships that the troops suffered, many western commanders followed Connor's tactic of using winter campaigns to locate and attack the Indians. Certainly army leaders recognized the colonel's victory as a major step toward peace. Commanding General Henry W. Halleck promoted him to the rank of brigadier general.

Apparently the Shoshonis also recognized that the massacre by the volunteers meant that they had to change their tactics. Now that the invading Americans had become so strong the Indians realized that they had to negotiate rather than fight. In the summer of 1863 Indian super-intendent James D. Doty, accompanied by Connor, ended the contest for control of the region between the Indians and the newcomers that had lasted for twenty-five years. The two men negotiated five treaties with the Indians there. These treaties offered presents, established reservations, provided annuities, and implied protection for the indigenous people.[26] While the new agreements did not settle all of the existing Indian-white disputes or totally end the sporadic violence that had marked the area, they brought a measure of peace for incoming settlers, travelers on the overland trail, and the Indians.

As a military exercise the Bear River fight proved far more successful than most engagements against the Indians. At least as bloody as later events at Sand Creek and Wounded Knee, it demonstrated clearly the effectiveness of winter attacks. During the rest of the year, mounted Indian raiders repeatedly simply outrode pursuing cavalrymen and continued their raids. As winter limited their mobility, the troops forced the villagers to stand and fight to protect their families and property. Colonel Connor's winter attack offered a striking example of how to defeat mounted Indians, and later commanders used the same tactic to achieve victory. At this scene the volunteer officers, unlike those under Colonel Harney at Ash Hollow, failed to prevent their men from committing numerous atrocities. The little known events at Bear River represented one of the bloodiest massacres of western Indians in American history.

CHAPTER 5

Sand Creek, 1864

As thousands of Americans poured west across the central plains during the early 1860s their actions brought repeated violent incidents similar to ones that travelers had provoked with the Shoshonis in Utah and Idaho. The mounted large and well-equipped hunting bands of Pawnees, Sioux, Crows, Cheyennes, Arapahos, and Comanches posed a serious threat to peace and safety for whites passing through their homelands. If anyone bothered to warn the immigrants of the possible danger, clearly most of them ignored that news as they moved west. Their actions led to misunderstandings, confrontations, suspicions, and interracial violence recalling the events on the Utah-Idaho stretch of the Overland Trail farther west. In Kansas, Nebraska, and Colorado too, indigenous people blamed the thousands of immigrants moving through their country for driving away the game and destroying the other resources that they needed for survival.

The situation at Sand Creek in Colorado resembled the circumstances leading to the 1863 Bear Creek Massacre in other ways. Both occurred in the West during the Civil War when Americans focused their attention on military events in the East. In each case the violence took place in lightly settled territories where local rather than federal officers directed Indian Affairs. People in each area depended on U.S. Volunteers not regular U.S. Army troops for their defense. Mostly recent arrivals to the West, these short-term soldiers shared their neighbors' fear and antipathy toward Indians. The volunteers served under Colonels Patrick Connor and John Chivington, both eager to build reputations as tough, effective commanders, whose job was to protect the western settlers. Pitted against them, the bands of militant Cheyenne Dog Soldiers refused to leave their prime hunting grounds along the Smoky Hill River in central Kansas. Clearly the 1864 massacre at Sand Creek shared many elements present at Bear Creek years earlier. The two incidents rank among the most vicious massacres in American history. Yet the attack at Sand Creek stood alone. It raised a firestorm of criticism and earned the label "massacre" from three federal investigations as part of its immediate aftermath.[1]

While the intruding pioneers caused much of the unrest, actions taken by frontier army officers, Colorado territorial officials, federal negotiators, and Indian militants defending their home territory caused repeated violence and tension. By 1848 the United States had extended its reach to the Pacific, prospectors had discovered gold in California, and the Overland, Mormon, and Santa Fe Trails all passed directly through the heart of Plains Indian country. This persuaded federal officials to sign treaties with local tribes in order to allow the peaceful movement of pioneers west. In 1851 the Cheyennes and Arapahos signed one of the agreements negotiated at Fort Laramie. This treaty, which the Indians called the Treaty of Horse Creek, recognized their home territory as reaching from western Kansas and Nebraska to the Rocky Mountains.[2]

As more immigrants trekked west, the army built new forts in former Indian country. Troops from these tiny outposts brought increasing violence and tension. The 1854 Grattan incident and General Harney's attack on a Sioux village at Ash Hollow the following year show the army's willingness to attack Indian camps clearly. The Cheyennes experienced repeated incidents with soldiers and pioneers that frightened and angered them. The first happened in April 1856, when a small party of Northern Cheyennes visited the area near the Upper Platte River bridge in eastern Wyoming. They came to trade, so they found four horses running loose, rounded them up, and took them back to their camp. Soon they learned that the owner would pay a reward if they returned his animals, so four of the men took three of the horses to the nearby army camp. When asked about the fourth horse, they said that they had left it behind because it had not been with the others and did not fit the owner's description. Rather than thanking the men for returning three of the animals, the officer in charge ordered his men to arrest the Indians and put them in leg irons until others returned the last horse.

The Cheyennes, who routinely killed their male prisoners, thought that the soldiers were about to kill them, so they tried to escape. In the confusion that followed the soldiers shot and killed one of the captives and wounded a second, who raced back to the Indian camp to warn them, and imprisoned the other two captives. One of the two prisoners soon died. The local commanding officer enraged the Indians when he refused to allow them to have the man's corpse for burial. Fearing that the troops might attack as General Harney had done at Ash Hollow, the Cheyennes fled just ahead of the troops, who looted and burned the now empty camp.[3] The officers had not charged the men with stealing the horses, so Indians considered this an unjustified attack rather than the thanks for their cooperation they had expected. The soldiers' unexpected reaction to an argument over a single horse illustrated a pattern of military overreaction to Indian actions on the plains for much of the next decade. With little or no evidence that tribal people had done anything wrong, officers rejected their explanations, refused to investigate the circumstances, and reacted violently to their actions.

In this situation of fear, mistrust, and violence some Indian actions did little to reduce tensions. The Treaty of Fort Laramie called on tribal leaders to stop their men from raiding. Tribal custom demanded retaliation for past enemy actions, however, so the ongoing pattern of raiding and retaliation continued. This led to minor incidents, suspicion, and more violence. In the late summer of 1856 a Cheyenne and Arapaho war party camped along the road to Fort Laramie. When the mail wagon for the fort passed their camp, several of the young men rode after it, trying to get some tobacco from the driver. He ignored them. When two of the Indians continued to beg, he panicked and began firing his pistol at them. The Indians returned fire with their bows and arrows, wounding him slightly in the arm. Realizing that this unexpected attack on a white man might bring a dangerous response, the chiefs whipped the two young men and left the area. The commanding officer at the fort send a party of forty-one cavalrymen after the Indians. When they found them the next day, the Cheyennes dropped their bows and arrows to show they wanted no fight, but the troopers attacked without any warning. After six of their men died, the Indians fled. The victorious whites seized their horses, and looted and burned everything in the camp.[4]

The soldiers' action angered and confused the Indians. To them it seemed like another unjustified attack. Following clan practices, they began retaliatory raids on white settlers and travelers passing through their country. The chiefs quickly intervened and sent messengers to Fort Laramie to explain what had happened. They reminded the officers at the fort that the two young men had only begged for tobacco and that the driver began the fight by firing his pistol. The chiefs asked Thomas Twiss, the Indian agent there, why the soldiers had shot at the Indians when they had laid down their weapons. Twiss had no good answer. The chiefs warned him that, even though they wanted peace, they could not stop the young men from retaliating for the soldiers' murder of their unarmed friends.[5]

Having failed to satisfy the chiefs, agent Twiss tried to persuade the army to stop its attack on the Plains tribes, but he got nowhere. In fact, General Persifor Smith, then commanding U.S. forces in the West, did the opposite. He ordered Colonel Edwin Sumner to punish the Cheyennes for their continuing raids. The colonel led a force of four hundred men west from Fort Leavenworth. On July 29 the two forces met at the Battle of Solomon's Fork. The three hundred mounted Cheyenne warriors faced about the same of army cavalrymen. But when the soldiers charged with their sabers, the startled warriors fled. The major result of the encounter occurred two days later, when Sumner's men destroyed the abandoned village with nearly all of the Indians' property, clothing, and food.[6] At that point some of the Indians clearly realized that the incoming whites were challenging their way of life.

That became clear after gold seekers flooded into the region set aside for the Cheyennes and Arapahos in the 1851 Treaty of Fort Laramie. Deciding how to deal with these people and other whites moving into or through their land fractured the tribal council of forty-four chiefs. The northern Cheyenne bands still moved across land between the North and South Platte Rivers and met fewer whites than their southern relatives. The southern bands encountered whites, who cut the trees along the streams, killed the buffalo, and occupied former Indian campsites. When disease and hunger swept through the Southern Cheyenne villages, it became clear that the tribe had to act. Despite the bitter differences separating chiefs of the northern, southern, and warrior bands, their new agent, William Bent, tried to get them together. In 1859 he reported that "a smouldering passion agitates these people, perpetually fomented by the failure of food [and] the encroachment of the white population. . . . A desperate war of starvation and extinction is therefore imminent and inevitable, unless prompt measures shall present it."[7]

Federal officials recognized that the miners pouring into Cheyenne country might bring violence. In August of 1859 the commissioner of Indian Affairs, Alfred Greenwood, traveled west to Bent's Fort to meet tribal leaders, not realizing that most of the villagers had not yet returned from their summer buffalo hunts. His visit attracted only four of the major chiefs from the southern bands. None of the Northern Cheyennes or the nearly independent soldier societies' leaders attended the treaty council, which doomed it from the start. By custom individual chiefs rejected any agreement that they had not signed and had no authority to force their band members to obey any treaty. To keep peace the commissioner urged his listeners to stop depending on hunting because it brought them into contact with the invading whites. He assured them that they would be safer if they became farmers and offered them $450,000 in treaty goods as payment for their accepting a much smaller land area than the earlier Treaty of Fort Laramie had assigned them. With no knowledge of the region, federal negotiators who wrote the Treaty of Fort Wise assigned their listeners to an area where they could not survive. It contained no sizable buffalo herds for hunting and lacked enough water for successful farming.[8]

While the 1861 Treaty of Fort Wise reduced the tribe's territory by at least 90 percent, it failed either to achieve American goals or to satisfy the Indians. Instead it showed clearly that Cheyenne society had changed dramatically. The northern and southern bands occupied separate regions and faced different issues. The northern groups lived primarily between the North and South Platte Rivers and along the Smoky Hill River and joined the Sioux hunting the still large buffalo herds there. At the same time, the southern bands moved across the country between the South Platte and Arkansas Rivers, where they met far more whites than their northern relatives did. The warrior bands lived with the northerners and refused to quit their summer hunting or to surrender their land to the whites. The southern bands faced more whites and could not depend on hunting to meet their needs, so the few chiefs who accepted agent Bent's invitation to the treaty council spoke for the people who hoped for peace. When they gathered to sign the treaty in February 1861, it promised annuities for fifteen years, a sawmill, and workshops as well as the services of interpreters, millers, farmers, and mechanics for five years. Black Kettle and five other chiefs who put their marks on the paper thought that it allowed them to continue their buffalo hunts off the new smaller home area, but that was not so. That would cause some dispute, as did the fact that thirty-eight of the forty-four chiefs had not participated in the negotiation and by their customs did not have to obey the new agreement.[9]

The outbreak of the Civil War in 1861 had an immediate impact on western Indian affairs. Desperate federal officials focused their attention on the devastating fighting in the East, not isolated incidents with indigenous people. Meanwhile, thousands of pioneers, miners, and ranchers continued to move into and through the prime hunting areas of the Plains tribes. In general, Indians did not go out of their way to treat the whites as enemies: they already faced enough indigenous enemies. Still, in virtually all tribes custom demanded retaliation for injuries to tribal members by outsiders passing through their country, and young warriors responded quickly. White and Indian violence led to an ongoing cycle of minor incidents, attacks, thefts, and occasional deaths. Americans repeatedly ignored or rejected Indian motivations or explanations, assuming that the Indians understood only force. U.S. military operations labeled the indigenous people as the aggressors and acted to punish them.

Just a year after the Treaty of Fort Wise John Evans became governor of Colorado Territory. Eager to get Indian land, he acted much like Andrew Jackson and other frontier leaders a half-century earlier when they dealt with the Creeks in Alabama. In Colorado he joined the business elite and quickly supported their land speculation, ranching, and mining activities. He called for a transcontinental railroad through Denver, hoping to move the territory quickly toward statehood. At the time some speculated that the governor hoped to become a U.S senator when Colorado became a state. Whatever his political plans, he saw Indian-held land as an obstacle to local economic growth. His statements and actions were aimed at pushing the Indians aside. He and other community leaders spread rumors of Indians carrying out violent attacks on immigrants traveling west even when no such incidents happened. Without local violence the leaders focused attention on far-away events such as the Minnesota War with the Dakota Sioux there.

Unable to point at any Cheyenne or Arapaho threat, the governor focused on their annual buffalo hunt as having a potential for violence and began trying to end it. Meanwhile, in the spring of 1863 agent Samuel Colley led a multitribal delegation to meet President Lincoln in Washington. Chief Lean Bear told the president that the Cheyennes wanted peace and asked him to stop the pioneers' attacks on the Indians. Lincoln responded, as most of his predecessors had, by urging his visitors "to become farmers."[10] Few of the assembled chiefs wanted to hear that message, and it is not clear that the visit changed their thinking or actions when they returned home.

By September Governor Evans and Colorado territorial military commander John Chivington had decided to enforce the Fort Wise Treaty provisions. In particular, the two leaders wanted the Cheyennes to stop their buffalo hunting that took them off their new reservation. Evans sent Eldridge Gerry, a local rancher, to the scattered hunting camps, urging them to return home and meet the governor on September 1 for a council. Few of the chiefs wanted to return home, because they were still hunting and needed the food for survival. So no Indians had arrived when the governor reached the rendezvous. Angry, Evans returned to Denver and sent Gerry back to learn why the Cheyenne leaders had boycotted the meeting. The chiefs gave him several excuses, but their main reason was that only a few of them had signed the treaty, so they saw no reason to obey its provisions. Their argument resembled the argument of the Sauks and Meskwakies after their 1804 treaty with William Henry Harrison. Like those tribes, most of the Cheyenne and Arapaho chiefs had not put their marks on the treaty and refused to stop hunting. Their most important reason for ignoring the treaty was that no buffalo lived on their new land, so they had to leave it to hunt the animals or face starvation.

The Cheyenne leaders who met Gerry said that they did not trust the whites to keep the peace. They reported angrily that an army guard at one of the forts had killed a tribal member after they had been told it was safe to visit and trade there. While the agent had given gifts to his family to honor the Indian practice of "covering the blood," his relatives rejected the presents. The chiefs warned that retaliation would continue. Furious about American military actions, they told Gerry that "the white man's hands are dripping with our people's blood, and now he [Governor Evans] calls for us to make a treaty!"[11] These comments showed the Indians' mood. Most of the chiefs had not signed the treaty. Along with the leaders of the warrior societies, they refused to move onto the reservation or to stop hunting.[12]

Whatever else the chiefs said to Gerry, he informed the governor that the leaders of the two tribes remained hostile. Evans took no action. But in November 1863 he heard rumors that all of the Plains tribes had formed an alliance and had agreed to attack the whites "as soon as the grass was up in the spring."[13] The governor found no evidence to support this charge, but he concluded that the Indians had to move onto their new treaty lands and that he might have to use troops to force them to obey the treaty. While Colorado leaders took no action. William Byers, editor of the *Rocky Mountain News*, filled the paper's pages with vicious rants about Indian savagery and the danger that the tribal people posed to the people in Denver. In one of his columns he depicted Indians as "a dissolute, vagabondish, brutal and ungrateful race" that "ought to be wiped from the face of the earth."[14] Byers continued to print articles featuring Indian attacks wherever they happened in the West, which helped fuel popular anti-Indian feelings.

In this situation Governor Evans's determination to gain clear title to much of the Cheyenne land in central Colorado echoed the motivations of other political leaders. To keep the peace Evans decided that he had to force the Cheyennes and Arapahos onto their new reservation. To accomplish that, he traveled to Washington in December 1863 to ask for troops, but political and military leaders there rejected his request. The troops had to remain in the East to fight Confederate forces.[15] While the governor traveled to the capital during the 1863–64 winter, the Indians faced starvation. They stole horses and cattle to feed their families. While their agent Samuel Colley reported that "most of the depredations committed by them are from starvation," he chided them for not understanding that "they have no right to take from them that have, when in a starving condition."[16] Despite the agent's report, the Cheyennes remained at peace and usually stayed away from the white settlements and ranches.

The situation changed drastically the next summer. Misunderstanding of Indian actions, Colorado militia aggressiveness, and a lack of interpreters repeatedly combined to ignite violence. In April 1864 government contractors reported that Cheyenne men had stolen a herd of their cattle. The Indians had found some of the herd wandering around and drove the animals to their village, apparently hoping for a reward for gathering the strays. Colonel John Chivington ordered Lieutenant George Eayre to recover the cattle and punish the men that the colonel considered thieves. At the head of 54-man detachment, the lieutenant set out after the Indians. Finding the trail of more than 100 cattle, he followed them to a village. Then, instead of halting to parley, the soldiers charged into the camp as the Cheyennes fled. Although the militiamen found no stolen cattle, they looted the abandoned lodges, taking buffalo robes, meat blankets, utensils, and anything else they could carry, and then burned everything else to the ground. Next the command found another deserted small village, which they also looted and destroyed.[17]

Having failed to destroy anything more than deserted villages, Eayre's men returned home. In mid-May he led another force looking for Cheyenne villages, in a campaign to "kill Cheyennes whenever and wherever found."[18] This time his troops found a larger camp than they expected, and their actions set off a series of raids and retaliations that spread terror across the central plains. The lieutenant led a force of 84 men up to the large 250-lodge village. When they saw the soldiers approaching, Chief Starving Bear and a few warriors rode out to meet the soldiers. The chief left his men behind. Wearing the peace medal that President Lincoln had given him earlier, he rode out to meet the soldiers. As he made peace signs, Eayre ordered the troops to fire: the bullets riddled Starving Bear. Enraged warriors raced down the hillside, firing as they rode. Soon as many as 500 Indians threatened to destroy the troops. At that point the peace chiefs intervened and managed to stop the fighting, allowing Eayre and his battered command to flee to safety.[19]

This pattern of incidents involving heavy-handed actions and unprovoked attacks destroyed any chance for peace on the central plains that summer. Colonel Chivington's orders to his unit commanders encouraged them to punish the Indians that they met. Unfortunately, the cavalrymen rarely located the hostile groups, so they attacked peaceful villages instead repeatedly, repeating a sad pattern in Western history. The actions of the volunteers, who were operating with limited knowledge, uncertain evidence, and few interpreters, tended to make matters worse. Their orders to recover stolen livestock, kill the thieves, and disarm the men all infuriated the villagers. The Indians reported that the troops attacked only innocent villages, that they were punished when they tried to help gather runaway livestock, and that the soldiers seized their weapons, which they needed in order to feed their families. While some bands of Northern Cheyennes and the warrior societies did raid ranches for livestock, the southern bands had tried to remain at peace. That gave the peaceful bands little protection, because white leaders failed to recognize the tribal divisions or chose to ignore them.

On June 11, 1864, a small party of Arapahos raided a farm occupied by Ward Hungate. They burned the family house to the ground and butchered Hungate, his wife, and two small daughters. The raiders mutilated Hungate's corpse and raped, scalped, and stabbed his wife, as well as killing and scalping the children. Apparently hoping to gain public support for their anti-Indian actions, the authorities brought the remains to Denver and displayed the bodies to the panicked citizens. News of the atrocity sent people fleeing into town from nearby ranches, spread fear, and brought demands for revenge. Colonel Chivington sent a company of volunteers after the raiders, but they had vanished.[20] This incident caused outrage in Denver and anti-Indian hatred that led directly to the late November massacre at Sand Creek that year.

On June 27, in what he claimed was an effort to "protect friendly Indians from being killed by mistake," Governor Evans issued a proclamation directing peaceful Indian groups to report to their agents. Although his call for the tribal people to stop hunting and return to their homes seemed to offer peace, he also said that "the war on hostile Indians will be continued until they are all effectively subdued."[21]

The proclamation had little impact. Most of the bands remained on the plains hunting, so few of them heard his call. Even if they responded and returned to the Fort Wise area, there was no certain way to tell which bands were peaceful and which were not. Some of the militants still called for retribution for the previous attacks. They had no reason to stop their raids or to expect friendly treatment if they settled near the forts. When few of the bands responded, the governor sent emissaries including the trader William Bent to discuss ending hostilities. At a council with the peace chiefs, they agreed to accept the governor's invitation, requested a prisoner exchange, and asked authorities to conclude a general peace with the other Plains tribes.[22]

Major Edward Wynkoop, the commanding officer at Fort Lyon, had a good relationship with Black Kettle and several other peace chiefs. He urged them to meet Governor Evans. On September 28 he led a delegation of chiefs to Camp Weld near Denver to confer with the governor. Rather than trying to calm the situation, Evans accused the chiefs of having made an alliance with the Sioux and various other tribes to drive the whites out of Colorado. Black Kettle and others protested that they had tried to remain at peace, but the governor refused to accept their claims of innocence. One of the chiefs insisted that they had remained peaceful, because there were so few buffalo to hunt that his people could not live without the annuities that the government gave them. Near the end of the council Evans told his visitors that whatever peace they could make "must be made with the soldiers, and not with me." At that point Colonel Chivington told the Indians that "my rule of fighting white men or Indians is, to fight them until they lay down their arms and submit to military authority." He urged them to submit to Major Wynkoop. Apparently the chiefs assumed that meant they had achieved peace.[23]

Thinking they would be safe near Major Wynkoop's post, Black Kettle and several chiefs set up a new village on Sand Creek about forty miles from Fort Lyon. One village of Arapahos moved close to the fort. The people came in to trade as well as to get their annuities, and the major issued rations to some of them. This humane treatment of the Cheyennes brought complaints that Wynkoop was feeding hostile Indians. On November 5, 1864, Major Scott Anthony arrived at Fort Lyon with orders that Major Wynkoop be relieved of command and return east to explain his actions. At a meeting with the chiefs the new commander told them that he could not sign any peace agreement, but his manner seemed to assure the Indians that his troops would not attack them.[24]

Anthony's troops did not attack, but on the evening of November 28, 1864, troops of the Third Colorado Cavalry reached Fort Lyon. Colonel Chivington described his plan to attack Black Kettle's camp. He considered the chief to be responsible for all of the Cheyennes and for their continuing raids and attacks. All the officers at the fort except for Major Anthony had supported Wynkoop's effort to keep peace and objected to the attack. Chivington overrode their concerns and ordered his troops to begin their march. They rode most of the night and arrived at Sand Creek early on the morning of November 29. When the villagers first heard the hoofbeats, they hoped that the sounds came a buffalo herd. But they soon realized that it was the sound of soldiers coming. Black Kettle put up a U.S. flag on a tall lodge pole as a sign of peace, but the attackers ignored it. They surrounded the village, attacking from several directions while the artillery poured grapeshot into the Indian lodges. The attackers fired into individual lodges, riddling the dead and dying, and tracked and killed the wounded, while scalping and mutilating everyone they could. About a hundred men, women, and children raced out of the village during the fighting and tried to burrow into the sand along the creek.

While the Indians defended themselves, the troops rampaged through the village, killing, scalping, butchering, mutilating, and raping the dying Cheyennes. As at Bear River, where Connor's men had hacked off body parts, taken scalps and strips of skin from their victims, and raped women as well as wounded and dying prisoners, the soldiers at Sand Creek had many victims to terrorize and destroy. So many men witnessed the atrocities that the news spread rapidly across the country. Sand Creek attracted more attention than all previous massacres in American history. Two congressional investigations and a third investigation conducted by the War Department all held hearings and came to the same conclusion. Their three published reports ("The Massacre of Cheyenne Indians," "The Chivington Massacre," and the "Sand Creek Massacre") all spelled out the details of the slaughter.[25]

Meanwhile, the citizens of Denver toasted the Sand Creek victors, who had returned bearing dozens of scalps that they displayed proudly in the town's bars and theaters. In January 1865 a local soldier murdered Captain Silas Soule, who had testified against Colonel Chivington. When three visiting congressmen conducted a hearing about Indian Affairs in the West at the Denver Opera House, they heard the pioneers' opinion. Senator James Doolittle described the Indians' growing desperation as the buffalo herds melted away. He asked the audience if the government should put Indians on reservations and teach them to farm and raise cattle or should exterminate them. In response "there suddenly arose such a shout . . . almost loud enough to raise the roof of the Opera House—'Exterminate them! Exterminate them!'" When he got back to

Washington, Doolittle reported that "while it may be hard to make an Indian into a civilized white man, it is not so difficult a thing to make white men into Indian savages."[26]

Governor Evans and Colonel Chivington, aided by the repeated and reckless charges of Indian attacks and barbarity carried in William Byers's *Rocky Mountain News,* had created real fear of Indian attacks in Denver. The divided nature of the Plains tribes, their diffuse leadership, and social customs related to raiding, warfare, and retribution all made it difficult to keep peace. The frequency of small local raids and the inability of federal officials to police the main overland trails or protect scattered ranchers and miners fearing Indian attacks exacerbated the problem. The disaster at Sand Creek occurred because the Civil War had disrupted and weakened an already creaky territorial system that encouraged frontier whites to invade indigenous peoples' homelands. The growing presence of white pioneers had negative impacts on Indian life. The frequent unwillingness to accept tribal groups as equals and as rational humans fueled the interracial conflicts, creating bitterness and hatred on all sides. That situation and the lack of firm control by the officers in command allowed genocidal actions to occur here as well as in the earlier victories at Bear River and Bad Axe.

Interview between Gen. Jackson & Weatherford, by John Reuben Chapin (engraver) and W. Ridgway (artist). Library of Congress, LC-DIG-ppmsca-32639.

Battle of Bad Axe, engraved by Henry Lewis. Library of Congress, LC-USZ62-90.

Ma-Ka-Tai-Me-She-Kia-Kiah or Black Hawk, a Saukie Brave. Philadelphia: Published by F. W. Greenough, 1838. Library of Congress, LC-DIG-pga-07527.

Little Thunder, Smithsonian Institution, National Anthropological Archives, gno3555.

General Patrick E. Connor.
Library of Congress,
LC-B813-2124 C.

Colonel John M. Chivington.
Denver Public Library,
Western History
Collection, z-128.

Washita Prisoners: The Indian Campaign—Prisoners Captured by General Custer, sketched by Theodore R. Davis. Library of Congress, LC-USZ62-117248.

General George Crook. Library of Congress, LC-BH826- 2600.

Dull Knife and Little Wolf, November 1973. History Nebraska,
RG1227-19-03.

Burial of the dead at the battle of Wounded Knee, SD. Library of Congress, LC-USZ62-44458.

CHAPTER 6

Washita River, 1868

At dawn on November 27, 1868, Colonel George Custer led the men of the Seventh Cavalry in an attack on the Cheyenne village led by Chief Black Kettle. Operating under orders from General Philip Sheridan, Custer's men were to move toward the Indian camps along the Washita River and "destroy their villages and ponies; to kill or hang all warriors, and bring back all women and children."[1] Catching the 250 unsuspecting villagers almost entirely by surprise, the troopers swept into the camp, exchanging fire with fleeing Indians running for their lives. Despite Custer's orders to capture not kill the women and children, Captain Edward Myers's men shot some of them. Most of the other noncombatants remained in the lodges, afraid of being treated as they had been at Sand Creek. Once they took control of the village, the troops killed the pony herd and confiscated or burned everything else there.[2]

This assault, just one day short of four years since the bloody attack on the same villagers at Sand Creek, resulted from the army policy of catching the Indians in their villages as General Harney had done so successfully at Ash Hollow a decade earlier. While it did not take place during the winter, this destruction of the Sioux village had served as a graphic example of how to defeat the often elusive Plains Indians: catch them in their villages and attack. At Ash Hollow and Sand Creek the soldiers killed women and children during the confusion of battle. When the

firing stopped, the soldiers had about thirty-five men killed or wounded
and the Cheyennes suffered about forty casualties.[3] Unlike the assaults by
the volunteers at Bear River and Sand Creek, the regular troops at the
Washita did not run amok, murdering, raping, or mutilating their victims. Yet they shot all of the wounded Indian men. But Custer ordered
his men to gather the women and children as prisoners to discourage
attacks on his force by the nearby Cheyenne and Arapaho villagers as his
men retreated from the battle scene.[4]

This second raid on Black Kettle's camp grew directly out of the events
that followed Sand Creek four years earlier. Each buffalo-hunting tribe of
the central plains included several semi-independent bands, which rarely
came together physically or politically. In theory a council of forty-four
chiefs met to direct tribal matters, but that rarely happened. In fact, the
Cheyenne society included three distinct parts. The northern bands had
moved north and more often traveled and hunted with the Sioux north
of the Platte River. The southern bands usually hunted south of the Platte
between it and the Arkansas River. While the military societies led by the
Dog Soldiers hunted along the Smoky Hill River. Chiefs in these three
divisions rarely cooperated with each other, and often the chiefs of the
northern and soldier bands defended their hunting area vigorously. They
repeatedly raided travelers, ranchers, stage and freight stations, and even
military posts in their territory. The southern bands, terrorized by the
vicious attack on Black Kettle's village at Sand Creek, remained more
nearly peaceful.

Those tribal divisions and the chiefs' inability to enforce any agreements made with the invading whites made the plains a dangerous place
at times. Angry hunters raided the increasing numbers of whites traveling through their prime hunting areas, who killed or frightened the
game that Indians needed for survival. Their animals ate the grass and
drank the water upon which the tribes' horse herds depended. Occasionally immigrants shot at the hunters or tried to take their guns, while
Indians tried to steal livestock from people moving west. Both sides
feared the other. Few Indians or whites spoke each other's language, so
minor incidents could create dangerous situations. The buffalo hunters
who came onto the plains after the Civil War enraged the tribal hunters
by killing tens of thousands of the animals and taking only their hides
and tongues while leaving the carcasses to rot on the prairie.

Like the Indian chiefs, American leaders quarreled over how to deal with potential Indian-white violence in the West. In 1849, when Congress created the new Department of the Interior, it moved the Office of Indian Affairs from the War Department to the civilian-run new department. With that shift civilian Indian agents now reported to the Department of the Interior rather than to the secretary of war. This added confusion in managing Indian Affairs: civilians drew up treaties and set policies for dealing with the tribes, while the War Department and the army had to keep peace in the West. Those conflicting or competing goals made dealing with the indigenous people more difficult than if a single agency had been in control. This resulted in disputes and misunderstandings that made negotiating and keeping peace on the central plains nearly impossible. Civilian and military officials differed over assigning blame for Indian raids. Army commanders usually rejected the idea that chiefs could not prevent individual warriors from leaving their villages to raid or steal livestock. Indian agents who knew band leaders personally often realized that the chiefs could not control the actions of their band members even though they may have wanted peace.

These differing views help to explain some of the incidents that occurred. When army commanders learned that raiders came from a particular village, they blamed the chiefs and labeled the group as hostile. At the same time, village leaders thought that they were not guilty of the raiding taking place because they had tried to keep peace. Military planners also thought that chiefs who signed a treaty spoke for the whole tribe. Because of the division of the Cheyennes into northern, southern, and warrior society bands with a council of forty-four chiefs, the Indians assumed that any agreement signed by fewer than all of the tribal leaders lacked validity. Moreover, the generals' adoption of the total war strategy that included destroying Indian housing, food, equipment, and horses through winter campaigns led to vicious assaults such as those at Sand Creek and the Washita River.

To understand Custer's raid at the Washita, we need to trace the actions of the Cheyenne and army leaders following the butchery at Sand Creek. In that attack the Colorado Volunteers had killed most of the Southern Cheyenne chiefs who had worked for peace. News of the unexpected attack spread quickly, so few Cheyennes or Arapahos would meet American negotiators or come to any of the forts. According to one observer, if any troops were near even "an angel from Heaven would not convince them but what another 'Chivington Massacre' was intended."[5] The slaughter at Sand Creek enraged many Plains Indians. It led some peaceful bands to join the militant Dog Soldiers in their raids to drive whites out of their prime hunting areas and against immigrants on the overland trails and the railroad surveys along the Smoky Hill River.

The government responded to the increased raiding by sending out two expeditions against the Sioux and Cheyennes, but neither found or punished any Indians. At the same time, Jesse Leavenworth persuaded the few remaining Cheyenne and Arapaho peace chiefs to negotiate a reparations treaty, which offered indemnities for damages and losses at Sand Creek. It offered each survivor who had lost husbands or parents individual plots of land as well as "animals, goods provisions, or . . . other useful articles." The treaty surrendered all Cheyenne claims to land between the Platte and Arkansas Rivers, some of the best buffalo hunting territory on the plains.[6] On October 14, 1865, Black Kettle and Little Raven signed this agreement. At the ceremony Black Kettle warned the commissioners that most of the Cheyenne bands had not signed or even seen the treaty and would not accept its conditions. The white negotiators responded that only the people at the council had to obey the new treaty provisions. Black Kettle told the commissioners that only the whites could bring peace. He complained that the whites broke their promises and attacked Indians repeatedly. "Your young soldiers, I don't think they listen to you. You bring presents, and when I come to get them I am afraid they will strike me before I get away."[7]

The nontreaty bands continued raiding on the central plains, probably unaware of the new treaty. Edward Wynkoop, who had known some tribal leaders before Sand Creek, became the new agent, with orders to get all Cheyenne bands to accept the move to the new treaty lands. In February 1866 he met with Dog Soldier leaders Big Head and Medicine Arrows, but both chiefs wanted to continue hunting north of the Arkansas River. After several meetings with the Dog Soldier leaders Wynkoop persuaded some of the chiefs to sign the treaty and promise to move into their new home area. It is likely that they did not realize what the new agreement demanded. Many of them balked when they realized that it required them to abandon their prime hunting area along the Smoky Hill River. Some of the most militant opponents of the new treaty threatened war if the whites tried to force them out of the Smoky Hill area. They even pressured Black Kettle to repudiate the treaty article surrendering that region. New raiding quickly began in that area, as agent Wynkoop worked frantically to bring peace. In November 1866 he persuaded the Dog Soldier leaders to accept the treaty.[8]

At this point army leaders took steps that worked directly against what the Indian Affairs officials had tried to accomplish. Major General Winfield Scott Hancock, in command of the Department of the Missouri, demanded that Cheyenne chiefs surrender the raiders who had killed whites and stolen livestock earlier that year. His call echoed those of General William Tecumseh Sherman, then commanding army units in the West. Sherman wanted to clear the Indians out of central Kansas and Nebraska to encourage settlement there. The continued raids there infuriated him. He raged that the tribes in the region "must be exterminated, for they cannot and will not settle down, and our people will force us to do it."[9] Whatever Hancock thought, in late 1866 he decided to move against the Cheyennes the next spring.

To prepare he ordered that that all traders and government agents stop selling or providing guns and ammunition to Indians on the central plains. The Indians immediately complained to their agents that their annuities included those items and that they needed the weapons for hunting to feed their families. The commissioner of Indian Affairs objected to the order, pointing out that existing laws allowed supplying guns to the tribes and that some of the treaty provisions included weapons as part of the annuities. Unmoved, Hancock turned to organizing his upcoming expedition. He expected to meet tribal leaders to determine whether the Cheyenne and Kiowa leaders wanted peace or war. In April 1867 his force of 1,400 men marched west. As the troops came near a large Indian camp, many people fled, afraid of another attack as at Sand Creek. The chiefs met Hancock, but he demanded that they bring the women and children back to their village. Fearing another Sand Creek, they delayed: soon all the Indians had fled. The general sent Colonel George Custer and the Seventh Cavalry after them, but they escaped. In retaliation Hancock ordered his men to burn all 300 lodges and their contents. Having failed to persuade, intimidate, or defeat the hostile groups, the general led many of his men back to Fort Leavenworth.[10]

Hancock's burning of the entire village enraged the warriors, who resumed raiding in the Smoky Hill area. They killed people, raped women, burned buildings, stole livestock, and spread terror, all of which the expedition was supposed to have prevented. Determined to punish the 200-man Cheyenne raiding party. General Philip Sheridan decided to strike back quickly. He chose Colonel George Forsyth to lead a command of about fifty hand-picked frontier scouts and experienced Indian fighters against the Cheyennes. If the whites could outshoot and outfight the Indians, they would be able to track and defeat larger Indian raiding parties. But this tactic failed. Forsyth and his men found more Cheyenne raiders than they had expected. The warriors' attack drove Forsyth's men onto a sandy island in the middle of the river. The combined force of Cheyenne, Arapaho, and Sioux fighters besieged the scouts for a week. By the time rescuers arrived in late September, the command was out of food, most of the horses were lost, and many of the scouts were dead or wounded.[11]

When news of Hancock's futile summer campaign reached Congress, it decided that the country was tired of war and that negotiations with the Plains tribes would cost less than fighting against them. On July 20, 1867, Congress created the Indian Peace Commission and assigned it the task of making peace with the warring tribes in the West. This decision put peace advocates and Office of Indian Affairs personnel in direct conflict with army leaders, who expected to pacify the region by demonstrations of American force. Chaired by the commissioner of Indian Affairs, Nathaniel Taylor, the group included generals Christopher Auger, Alfred Terry, and William Harney as well as senators John Henderson, Samuel Tappan, and John Sanborn. When the commissioners arrived at Fort Larned in Kansas, the Indians asked them to move the council site to Medicine Lodge Creek. The talks began on October 19, after all five of the major southern tribes had arrived: the Comanches, Kiowas, Kiowa Apaches, Cheyennes, and Arapahos.

The commissioners promised schools, homes, and farming equipment when the Indians moved to their new homes. Many of the peace chiefs who attended some part of the talks seemed to accept the idea that they had to surrender some of their land and move south to reservations in Indian Territory, but others objected.[12] They told the government negotiators that they wanted to continue their buffalo hunting in the Smoky

Hill River area and asked for guns and ammunition to continue doing so. Buffalo Chief spoke for the Dog Soldiers and signaled their unwillingness to move south. He described the region north of the Arkansas River as the place "where the bones of our fathers lie buried" and rejected the presents being offered. "You give us presents and then take our land— that provokes war," he said.[13] When other leaders echoed this objection to moving south, the commissioners told them that they could continue to hunt outside the reservation as long as the buffalo lasted. In late October 1867 the chiefs signed the new agreements: the Indians moved away to their winter camps.[14] Several eyewitnesses of the negotiations objected that the commissioners had not read the full treaties to the chiefs, so they had little idea of what the agreements really said.

That same autumn a significant change in western military commands placed Major General Philip Sheridan in charge of the Department of the Missouri, which oversaw all the central plains. The new commander had practiced total war in his Shenandoah Valley campaign near the end of the Civil War and brought that strategy west in his dealings with the Indians. In his view, the more he threatened the property and the women and children in each village, the sooner the fighting would end. The general's ideas were nothing new. Andrew Jackson's troops had destroyed entire Indian villages as early as the 1813 Red Stick War. Sheridan did not take his new command in the West until spring of 1868, but circumstances on the plains soon led to renewed hostilities. Whites moving into or through central Kansas complained that large bands of Indians still hunted there. At the same time, although officials delivered the promised annuities to the Cheyenne hunters, few of the promised guns or ammunition that the Indians needed for hunting arrived. In August 1868 a Cheyenne war party raided several isolated farms, killing the men, raping the women, and kidnapping children. General Sheridan reported thirteen murders and multiple rapes.[15]

Although few whites realized it, many of the Plains Indians were destitute, some near starvation. That certainly explains why even the peace-seeking villagers stole livestock. They needed to eat. The Medicine Lodge treaties had promised food, but the Senate failed to ratify the treaties until late 1868, delaying the annuity payments for months while the Indians went hungry. Commissioner Nathaniel Taylor pleaded with the Senate to hurry "to relieve the present wants of the most destitute, and to prevent another Indian war."[16] Yet at the same time he opposed issuing weapons or ammunition to the hunters when he learned of the new raids. His superior, the secretary of the interior, directed agent Edward Wynkoop to give the Cheyennes guns if he could do it without causing more violence. The agent issued the weapons quickly and reported being "perfectly satisfied that there will be no trouble with them [the Cheyennes] this season."[17] Clearly he was wrong.

As often happened in white-Indian affairs, both the Indians and the pioneers acted aggressively: violence continued. For example, when a member of a war party on its way to attack the Pawnees stopped at a farm to ask for food, the family started shooting at him. A day later the same raiders met a party of whites, who started shooting at them. Infuriated by the unprovoked attacks, the Cheyennes moved to other settlements: they killed 110 people, raped 13 women, stole more than 800 animals, and destroyed property.[18] The whites had no idea that other settlers had started the violence and saw the Indian actions as unprovoked attacks. The raids that followed spread terror in the newly settled areas and reflected the Indians' resentment and anger at having their way of life threatened by the invading whites. Ignoring the earlier incidents, General Sheridan stated that "there was not the slightest provocation offered by the soldiers or citizens" for these latest raids by the Cheyennes.[19] He called for the raiders "to be soundly whipped, and the ringleaders in the present trouble hung, [and] their ponies killed."[20]

While doing this Sherman and Sheridan expected to drive the raiding bands away from the settlements and force them south of the Arkansas River. As he planned operations General Sheridan reported that he wanted "to make war on the families and stock of these Indians," which would cause the Dog Soldiers and other raiders to move to protect their families.[21] His troops would cause the most misery if they destroyed the lodges, clothing, food, and animals of each village during the winter, when bad weather made living conditions harsh. Basically, he saw the village women and children as contributing to the raiding by processing food and providing shelter. In effect he proposed treating them as targets, the way modern governments have treated civilian workers in defense industries. Objecting to this policy, Indian Affairs officials urged Sheridan to distinguish between the villages led by chiefs seeking peace and those of the Dog Soldiers, but he refused. He argued that even the peace chiefs admitted that they could not prevent all the young men from slipping away to join the raiding bands and then returning to their home village later. This meant that each of the Indian bands became potential targets for surprise attacks.

In September 1868 Sheridan began his plan to punish the Cheyennes for their continuing raids. He moved to reinstate Colonel George A. Custer to active duty, placed him in command of the Seventh Cavalry, and gathered troops and supplies at Camp Supply in Indian Territory. At the same time the Arapaho chiefs Big Mouth and Black Kettle (leading spokesman for the peaceful Cheyenne bands) visited Fort Cobb along the Washita, hoping to avoid war. While Black Kettle had tried to keep the young men out of the fighting, he admitted that "some will not listen, and I have not been able to keep them home. But we all want peace."[22] The two chiefs asked Colonel William Hazen to protect them when they camped near the fort. He knew that General Sheridan had labeled these bands as hostile. Hazen was worried that he might be at the center of another Sand Creek Massacre if troops attacked the villagers while they camped nearby under his protection. So he refused to promise them sanctuary. Instead he told the chiefs that "General Sheridan, [is] the great war chief . . . and with him you must make peace."[23]

Disappointed, the chiefs led their bands to new camps along the Washita River, where they joined bands of Arapahos, Comanches, Kiowas, and Prairie Apaches whose villages clustered near the river, bringing as many as 6,000 people together there.[24] Apparently their leaders' failure to get a promise of safety from Colonel Hazen encouraged some of the truculent young men to ignore their chiefs' warnings. Instead of avoiding new raids, they urged other villages to begin war, predicting that "next spring the Sioux and other northern bands were coming down and would clean out this entire country."[25] It is unclear whether that prediction persuaded many of the young men to leave their villages and join the raiding parties on the plains, but those groups continued their attacks on both civilians and the soldiers pursuing them.

Sheridan's first big move against the tribes south of the Arkansas River began on September 7, when General Alfred Sully led the Seventh Cavalry and several companies of infantry in a new campaign against the Indians. His command depended on a long line of supply wagons, which proved difficult to get through the sandy hills, so the troops moved slowly. As the soldiers plodded ahead, small groups of Indian raiders harassed them repeatedly, shooting at the guards, capturing stragglers, and threatening to steal livestock. At one point the attackers, using signals from a bugle, charged the column repeatedly. Unable to match the Indians' mobility or to move close enough for any major fighting, Sully led the dispirited troops back to Fort Dodge. Their failure to locate any village or punish the raiders seems to have persuaded the Indians that the soldiers were too slow to catch them and convinced General Sheridan that a winter campaign offered the only chance to find and defeat the hostile groups.[26]

Disgusted with Sully's ineffective campaign, General Sheridan turned to his trusted subordinate George Custer, newly appointed as commander of the Seventh Cavalry. The two equipped the horse soldiers with new rifles, pistols, and cold-weather clothing, loading supplies for thirty days into the wagons that would follow the troops. The commander hired Osage warriors as scouts to serve with the white guides as the force prepared to begin its expedition. Sheridan ordered Custer's command "to proceed south . . . towards the Washita River . . . [and] to destroy their villages and ponies; to kill or hang all warriors, and bring back all women and children."[27] The men left Fort Dodge in freezing weather as they crossed the snow-covered plains en route to the Washita.

Early on November 26 Custer's men came across the fresh trail of a hundred-man raiding party, which they followed through the snow until well after midnight. After the Osage scouts found a village, Custer had his men rest for a few hours. Just before dawn he divided the troopers into four columns in order to surround and destroy the village. When the trumpeters sounded "charge" at dawn, the troops raced into Black Kettle's camp, catching the Indians almost entirely by surprise. As the villagers ran in all directions, the charging cavalrymen shot at anything that moved, killing and wounding men, women, and children. Within ten minutes the soldiers controlled the village, but the shooting continued as the scattered Indians fought to defend themselves from behind trees or in a nearby ravine. Some fled to the riverbank, where the troopers killed all they could find. Despite Custer's orders, Captain Edward Myers ordered his men to shoot the women and children they saw. During the fighting, many of the women and children hid in their lodges, making it easy for the soldiers to capture them once the firing stopped. One of the

Cheyenne women recalled that when the shooting began "we all ran out of our tepees." When the battle was over, "the next thing I knew a soldier punched me with his gun and motioned me to get up. . . . Men, women, and children lay dead everywhere."[28]

As always, the casualty figures depended on who made the count and when. Custer, like many battlefield commanders, exaggerated the Indian deaths and casualties. Initially he claimed to have killed 103 men and admitted that "in the excitement of the fight, as well as in self-defense, it so happened that some of the squaws and a few children were killed or wounded."[29] Several weeks later he wrote that the Indians had confirmed that 140 men had been killed in the attack, along with many others wounded: when this number was added to the prisoners taken, the Cheyenne loss came to nearly 300 people.

Custer clearly exaggerated the casualties, because the village included only fifty-one lodges, with an estimated five people in each. Several of the scouts reported fewer casualties. One estimated the Cheyenne loss "at seventy-five warriors and fully as many women and children killed." Another wrote that "the Indians lost five chiefs and distinguished braves . . . and about 75 of their ordinary fighting men were killed."[30] Later interviews with Indians indicated that the Cheyennes admitted that thirteen men, sixteen women, and nine children died in the fight.[31]

Several weeks later General Sheridan sent another force back to the Washita. After passing through the remains of Black Kettle's camp, they reported finding the bodies of several women and children, wrapped in blankets and prepared for burial, as well as another thirty corpses in the nearby hills, adding to the total for Indian casualties.[32] The Indians taken prisoner reported that 16 men had been killed, but they had not seen all of the dead.[33] Custer's command suffered 20 men killed and 13 wounded, which shows how effective the unexpected attack had been.[34] Once Cheyenne resistance ended, the troopers killed the village pony heard of 875 animals, destroyed all 51 lodges, and burned 1,100 buffalo robes, 470 blankets, clothing, dried meat and other stored food, weapons and ammunition, and whatever else they found. Essentially that morning they obliterated Black Kettle's village.[35]

While Custer gained a crushing victory over Black Kettle's band, his men faced possible defeat and annihilation: hundreds of warriors from the nearby Cheyenne, Arapaho, and Kiowa camps rode toward the battle.

Soon Custer saw armed warriors on the nearby hills looking down at his command. He realized that with the corpses of the dead soldiers, the wounded, and the prisoners he would have to forget about assaulting the other camps and lead the troops to safety. By evening the command had packed its equipment, gathering the dead and wounded men, and began to leave the scene. Instead of retreating, Custer led the troops in a feint toward the other villages. The warriors who had threatened to attack his column earlier raced back to their home villages to move them away from the soldiers. Once that happened, the commander led the exhausted regiment back toward their supply train, using the captive women and children as a shield against further Indian attacks. From there they returned to Camp Supply without seeing any more Indians.[36] There General Sheridan praised Custer's victory and predicted that "if we can get one or two more good blows there will be no more Indian troubles in my Department." He made plans for another campaign.[37]

While the secretary of war and General Sherman both applauded the Washita victory, others objected, likening it to Sand Creek: it was just another army attack on a peaceful Indian village. For some months military leaders and civilian critics exchanged charges against and defenses of the attack on Black Kettle's camp. The army officers claimed that the chief had rejected General Hazen's invitation to move his people to Fort Cobb. Indian agent Edward Wynkoop explained that the chief's decision was due to his experience at Sand Creek four years earlier. Commissioner Nathaniel Taylor debunked General Sheridan's charge that the large raiding party that Custer's force had trailed was even Cheyenne. He reported that a Kiowa chief had explained that a Kiowa raiding party trying to attack the Utes had stopped briefly at Black Kettle's village: it was their trail that Custer's scouts had found. News of the attack brought a protest from the Cherokee, Creek, and Choctaw tribes, describing the attack as "a brutal massacre of friendly Indians" and calling for an investigation.[38] Even retired General William Harney defended the chief, saying that "I know Black Kettle was as good a friend of the U.S. as I am."[39]

The criticisms of Custer's attack enraged General Sheridan, who complained bitterly to General Sherman. In support of the raid he wrote that Custer had reported that his troops had "secured two white children, held captive by the Indians. One white woman who was in their possession was murdered by her captors the moment we attacked."[40] Later investigation showed that the first claim was false: the troops failed to find any captive white children. However, they found the body of Clara Blinn, who had been shot in the back of the head, and her murdered son Willie.[41] Sherman reminded his angry subordinate of having sent President Grant plenty of evidence to justify the Washita attack. He encouraged his officers: "Pay no attention to the furor raised. This you know is a free country, and people have the right to misrepresent as much as they please, and to print" their ideas too.[42]

In his careful study of this incident Jerome Greene addresses the dispute over whether it was a massacre or just another bloody fight in a campaign based on the total-war doctrine. He concludes that it had elements of both.[43] The incident illustrated the ongoing bitter dispute between the army and the War Department on one side and humanitarians and the civilian employees of the Office of Indian Affairs on the other. The sharply differing views on how to treat the Indians by held people in the East and in the West brought continued death and destruction as they complicated American Indian affairs during the last half of the nineteenth century.

CHAPTER 7

Marias River, 1870

Whatever defense General Sheridan made for Custer's 1868 attack on the Cheyenne village on the Washita River, he could offer little to deflect criticism of the massacre of a Piegan camp on the Marias River in Montana two years later. Along with the fighting in the much earlier Red Stick War and at Sand Creek, this 1870 destruction of Chief Heavy Runner's camp ranks as one of the most violent and destructive assaults on an Indian village during the nineteenth century. In this incident the troops destroyed the wrong village and murdered eight of their prisoners when the fighting ended. Although it resulted from many of the same factors that led to the other attacks, the Montana situation had several distinctive features. First, it occurred near the boundary between Canada and the United States. What the Indians called the "Medicine Line" separated the two nations, creating an area where American whiskey traders gave the Indians plenty of alcohol. North of the line Hudson's Bay Company employees willingly bought stolen horses from the Indians. When the thieves drove herds of stolen animals into Canada, white ranchers had no way to recover their animals. Both these activities kept circumstances in the region unsettled and led to repeated minor incidents among Indian groups as well as between local whites and the tribal peoples.

The Blackfoot Confederacy included multiple bands of Blackfeet, Blood, and Piegan people. All of these groups lived in semi-independent villages and had their own chiefs. Because they lived in an area with long harsh winters and short growing seasons, these people raised no crops. Instead they hunted and traded to meet their needs. Like their Sioux and Cheyenne neighbors, they had no recognized spokesperson who could deal with American officials with any authority. Band and village chiefs might agree to cooperate with federal officials, but they could not prevent warlike young men from raiding enemy tribes or whites, horse stealing, or other violent acts. At the same time, the invading pioneers— mostly miners—had little use for Indians. Their aggressive actions kept the region in turmoil. When individual Indian men sought revenge for mistreatment by the whites because of Blackfeet customs, their actions led the intruding pioneers to retaliate.[1] Hoping to open a route for a northern transcontinental railroad and pacify the area, in October 1855 Washington territorial governor Isaac Stevens negotiated a treaty that set out the tribes' home territories and promised annuities for each band.[2] His effort failed to end Indian depredations, because the promised items for the Indians rarely met their needs. They had no use for flour, found rice too sticky, dumped the sugar on the ground, and thought the coffee tasted bitter. Instead of incorporating these things into their diet, they traded much of their annuity goods to the local whiskey dealers for things more to their liking.[3]

Stevens's effort to secure peace by means of treaties failed. The situation mirrored events across much of the West. Invading whites killed the game that Indians needed for survival. When tribal raiders stole horses, mules, or other livestock to replace the missing buffalo and other animals, the whites protested. Throughout the nineteenth century most of the invading whites viewed the indigenous people as dangerous "savages" and obstacles to progress and economic development. As white miners poured into Montana after the 1862 gold discoveries, every incident received wide public attention. Many westerners repeatedly called on the government to exterminate their Indian neighbors. Whatever Blackfeet band leaders or village chiefs said to government officials, they could not prevent the young men from raiding and isolated acts of violence. Those incidents incensed the pioneers. According to one author, "it was their fury over native horse theft that drove some whites to commit unspeakable acts of violence."[4] Indian custom demanded retribution for white actions, leading to a cycle of raids and responses.

While the 1862 gold discovery at Bannock was luring hundreds of miners to Blackfeet country, the Civil War drew attention away from Indian matters in all parts of the West. Local agents came and went, and the few soldiers manning the isolated army garrisons in the region could do little to keep peace. Worried that the incoming whites would try to take their land away from them, village chiefs objected to this invasion. When asked about new land cessions, they told their agent Henry Reed that they would not surrender any because the region "had been their home as well as that of their fathers, and they hoped to make it the place of their graves and the home of their children." Though nobody openly threatened their land title, the presence of hundreds of white men whom the agent described as not "be[ing] tolerated in any civilized society" had the potential for violence.[5] Predicting that an increased flood of alcohol into the region would further complicate matters, he called for the army to station several companies of troops at Fort Benton.

As the Civil War was ending in early 1865, a raiding party of Blood warriors stole forty horses at Fort Benton on April 23. A few weeks later local whites responded by killing four Indians who came to town to trade. Just a few days after that, on May 25, Blood chief Calf Shirt and a large war party met ten white members of a woodcutting detail near Fort Benton. According to the chief, the Indians signed that they were peaceful, but the timber cutters panicked and started shooting. That prompted a Blood attack in which the warriors killed all ten whites, stripped the corpses, and scalped one of the dead.[6]

After this incident territorial governor Thomas Meagher called for the federal government to extinguish Indian title to much of Montana and to push the Blackfeet bands away from the settlements. In November 1865 he and treaty negotiators persuaded tribal leaders to surrender some of their land. At first glance the new agreement seemed to gain what the governor wanted. Yet he knew enough about the Indians to realize that the few chiefs who put their marks on the paper lacked real any power to end the raiding. His misgivings had no impact, because news of renewed white-Indian clashes persuaded the commissioner of Indian Affairs to oppose the treaty: the Senate never ratified it. Colonel Alfred Sully, serving as superintendent of Indian Affairs in Montana, reported that the isolated Indian raids posed a major threat to the settlers and asked for more troops to protect them, but General Sherman ignored his request.

Sully cautioned that the miners had threatened to organize their own militia and punish the Crows and Blackfeet.[7]

Continuing violent incidents kept people in the area worried. During the winter of 1865–66 four Piegan young men visited the home of John Morgan. When they arrived, Morgan and several nearby prospectors captured the Piegans at gunpoint. They shot one of them and hanged the other three from a tree in the yard. Some Indian hunters witnessed the incident and hurried to bring the news to their chiefs. In April 1866 Chief Bull Head led a large party looking for revenge. The raiders attacked and destroyed the remains of the failed tribal farm and then turned their attention to the nearby Jesuit mission, killing some cattle and the animals' herder. Their raid frightened the missionaries, who blamed the settlers for starting the violence and abandoned their work among the Blackfeet. A month later the angry warriors attacked and killed Chief Little Dog and his son because they had been too friendly with the whites.[8]

Unlike some other frontier Indian wars, the conflict with the Blackfeet never expanded into a large area or included large numbers of fighters. It became a series of scattered and usually small-scale raids that continued to worry the settlers like a festering sore, not fatal but dangerous. As in the other mounted Plains societies, young men sought to prove their bravery with horse stealing and small-scale raids on neighboring tribes and the increasing numbers of whites in the area. When Governor Meagher described the scattered incidents as an Indian war, Augustus Chapman, the Flathead Indian agent, described his calls for help as "the biggest humbug of the age . . . to make a raid on the United States treasury."[9] In fact the agent reported that small groups of whites who traveled between Helena and Fort Benton were in no more danger from Indian attacks than if they had been in the national capital.

The agent's positive comments overlooked the continuing minor incidents taking place. In a clear signal that others did not share his views, in 1867 the U.S. Army established two new Montana forts, Fort Shaw and Fort Ellis. That same year raiders killed John Bozeman, founder of the trail into the gold fields that bore his name. The Indians objected to the new military outposts and complained that the government had not lived up to its 1865 treaty promise of increased annuities. The expected goods never arrived, because the Senate had failed to ratify the treaty. Blackfeet chiefs had no understanding of the treaty-making process and no one had explained it to them, so they assumed that the whites had lied. Hence they ignored their earlier promises to halt the raids. When the chiefs explained their actions, the Office of Indian Affairs decided to negotiate yet another agreement and in 1868 called for another meeting with the Blackfeet chiefs. In September they gathered at Fort Benton and reached a new agreement that repeated many of the earlier terms, set out tribal boundaries, and offered annuities to each band. Unfortunately, the Senate failed to ratify this agreement too, so again the unfulfilled promises increased misunderstandings and tension.[10]

The local commanding officer, Colonel Philippe Régis de Trobriand, had opposed Alfred Sully's earlier request for a military response because he saw that it would be almost impossible to identify which band of Indians had done the raiding and feared that innocent people might be assaulted. If the army attacked the wrong band, he predicted widespread but unnecessary raiding.[11] But he had no authority to halt the violence, so continuing incidents kept tempers on edge. In the summer of 1869 two events just a day apart triggered more violence and led directly to a new round of hostilities. The first was the murder of Malcolm Clarke, a former fur trader and successful rancher. Married to a Piegan woman, he knew their language and had many contacts within the tribe. On August 17, 1869, Owl Child and several other Indians came to the ranch. Owl Child was the cousin of Clarke's wife, so the family knew him well and welcomed the visitors for a late dinner. After the meal and without warning one of the Indians shot Clarke while Owl Child crushed his skull with an axe.[12]

Then thirty or so Piegans entered the house, trashed the kitchen, destroyed stores of food, and rode off with Clarke's cattle. At the time the attack surprised and puzzled people, but it resulted from a deep personal insult that Clarke had given Owl Child two years earlier. Owl Child and his family had been guests at the ranch. The Indians claimed that their host had raped Owl Child's wife while he was away hunting. When the Piegans left, they stole several of the ranch horses. Clarke and his son followed the Indians to their camp, where he reclaimed the animals and whipped the young Indian, calling him a thief and humiliating him in front of the other villagers. According to Piegan accounts, Owl Child brooded about this personal insult for two years before murdering

Clarke. The rancher's death shocked the settlers, who assumed that Clarke should have been safe because of his close personal connections with the Indians. Panic spread: fearing an all-out attack, they called on the army to punish the guilty.[13]

The second incident took place immediately after Clarke's murder. In a direct response to it, a gang of whites in Fort Benton murdered two Piegan men, including the elderly brother of Mountain Chief. After killing them, the whites threw their corpses into the Missouri River. Earlier Mountain Chief had told Malcolm Clarke, "I despise all whites; they have encroached on our territory; they are killing our buffalo, which will soon pass away; they have treated my nation like dogs," and he refused to try to halt the raids.[14] When the Piegans responded with new attacks, General Sully reported that "I fear we will have to consider the Blackfeet in a state of war" with the settlers. When he learned about the renewed Indian problems in Montana, Commanding General William T. Sherman responded: "The same Indians, the same men, and the same stories."[15] Despite his reluctance, he ordered Sheridan to plan for military operations. Sheridan, in turn, chose Major Eugene M. Baker of the Second Cavalry, a well-known subordinate from Civil War days, to take command of the move.[16]

Responding to the firestorms of criticism that had followed news of Sand Creek, Custer's attack on Black Kettle's village at the Washita, and what happened in Montana, Sheridan later defended using winter attacks on Indian villages. He told General Sherman that "I have to select a season when I can catch the fiends": if the troops hurt women and children, that was just the nature of war. "During the [Civil] war did anyone hesitate to attack a village or town occupied by the enemy because women or children were within its limits?" he asked. "Did we cease to throw shells into Vicksburg or Atlanta because women or children were there?"[17] The obvious answer was no. Still, to avoid another public relations disaster Sheridan ordered his Inspector Colonel James Hardie to examine the situation in Montana. There he met with Colonels Sully and de Trobriand, and with Blackfeet agent Lieutenant William B. Pease. Sully opposed an attack, while de Trobriand supported one. In mid-January 1870 Hardie agreed and recommended a winter campaign. Sheridan approved. He chose Major Baker to lead the attack and wired that "if lives and property of the citizens of Montana can best be protected by Striking Mountain Chief's band, I want them struck. Tell Baker to strike them hard."[18]

While the army began preparing for a winter campaign, U.S. Marshal William Wheeler had presented Colonel Sully with a grand jury indictment listing eighteen Piegans as responsible for Clarke's murder and demanded that the chiefs surrender the men responsible for that killing and the theft of several hundred horses. Sully forwarded Wheeler's message to the commissioner of Indian Affairs and got orders to demand that the Blackfeet chiefs capture the guilty men and turn them over to him. If they refused, he was to threaten them with a military attack. This effort had little chance to succeed. When the whites met the chiefs on January 1, 1870, only four of the nonhostile leaders appeared. He warned them that if they did not turn over the murderers to him within two weeks American leaders planned to invade Blackfeet country and impose peace. He threatened that if the chiefs failed to surrender the guilty men and end the raiding in Montana U.S. troops would pursue them over the border into Canada. Sully's threats had no impact, because the peaceful chiefs had no way to meet the demands: the effort to avoid war failed.[19]

In January 1870 Major Baker began his campaign when the negotiators failed to meet with the hostile Blackfeet leaders. After receiving General Sheridan's orders to "strike them hard," Colonel de Trobriand ordered Major Baker to lead his four companies of cavalrymen from Fort Ellis to Fort Shaw "with the least possible delay."[20]

When the major got there on January, he discussed the operation with both Colonel de Trobriand and Colonel Hardie. At Fort Shaw he added two companies of infantry to his force, mounting one company of the foot soldiers. He also hired two local scouts, Joe Kipp and Joseph Cobell. Both men knew the Piegans and the area well. For several days the command loaded its wagons with supplies as the men got their personal equipment and ammunition ready.[21]

Worried that the Indians would hurry across the Canadian border if they learned about the campaign, Colonel de Trobriand demanded absolute secrecy. Wearing blankets and buffalo robes over their uniforms to protect them from the bitter cold and to muddle the noise that they made, Baker's column moved out of Fort Shaw on January 19, marching in the bitter below-zero cold. After the first day the troops moved only at night to avoid being discovered. With the temperature dropping to thirty degrees below zero, the soldiers had to eat cold food because Major Baker feared that the Indians might see any fires they lit to cook their food. On January 22 they reached the Marias River, where several groups of Piegans had camped.[22]

Major Baker's orders directed him to attack the followers of Mountain Chief and to avoid any harm to the friendly band led by Chief Heavy Runner. After marching that night, the scouts found a small camp. The frightened Indians told them that Mountain Chief's camp stood another few miles down the Marias. At daybreak on September 23 the troops reached the banks of the Marias, where they found two camps totaling thirty-seven lodges. As they prepared for their attack, nobody was to speak or make any noise. The cavalry dismounted, with every fourth man holding the horses to free three of their companions for the attack. The other men lined the steep bluffs along the stream. From their positions they had a clear view of the nearby camps.

Just before Major Baker gave the order to begin firing, the scout Joe Kipp ran up shouting that this was Chief Heavy Runner's camp not Mountain Chief's camp, the intended target. Baker, furious that Kipp had ignored his order to remain quiet, threatened to arrest the scout, but his warning had aroused the sleeping Indians. Chief Heavy Runner ran out of his lodge, waving the good conduct paper that Colonel Sully had given him. As he neared the soldiers, a single shot rang out, killing him instantly. Years later scout Joe Cobell admitted to having killed Heavy Runner to start the attack and protect the downriver camp of Mountain Chief, a relative of his wife.[23]

Hearing the shot, the soldiers assumed that it was the signal to start firing and began shooting into the village. At least 200 men poured heavy fire into the lodges, at any Indian men trying to flee, and at the ties that held the hides to the lodge poles. When the teepees collapsed, their heavy coverings trapped those inside. Some people in the wreckage of the burning lodges died from suffocation or smoke inhalation. The firing continued for an hour. When resistance ended, Baker ordered his troops to stop shooting. At that point the mounted soldiers dashed into the village with pistols and sabers drawn. They hacked at lodges still standing, used lariats to pull them down, and fired into tents where Indians still tried to defend themselves. The infantrymen combed the riverbank and the nearby brush for escapees and pulled the terrified women and children out of the collapsing lodges. An Indian boy taken captive as the attack began remembered that the soldiers shot the survivors as they tore down the remaining lodges and tried to burn the corpses in the wreckage of the fallen lodges.[24] Recalling the attack, Lieutenant Gustavus Doane describe it as the "greatest slaughter of Indians ever made by U.S. troops."[25]

When they rounded up 140 survivors, mostly women and children, the troops realized that smallpox had hit the village. Although they were vaccinated, they worried about spreading the disease, so they turned their captives loose. Major Baker ordered that some hardtack and bacon be left to keep the villagers from starving and then moved most of the troops away from the ruined camp. A few soldiers remained to guard the men who had survived. That evening eight of them tried in vain to escape. The soldiers recaptured them, leading to a grisly atrocity. Lieutenant Doane ordered his men to execute the recaptured escapees. When they prepared to shoot the prisoners, one witness heard Doane say: "No, don't use your guns. . . . Get axes and kill them one at a time." Bear Head, one of the survivors, was only six at the time of the event. He claimed to have heard Doane's order, followed by "a sound as if someone was cutting up meat with an axe and a Grunt." In the firelight he saw one of "the Indians lying on the ground with his head split open."[26]

The victorious troops returned to Fort Shaw on January 2. An excited Colonel de Trobriand reported the victory to General Sheridan. He praised Baker for the raid and concluded: "I am confident that peace and security is secured for a long time in the Territory."[27] Yet from the start details of the attack and its results varied widely. The only figures that the reports agreed on was that 173 Piegans had died in the early morning fight. When they buried the dead, the Indians claimed that they buried only 33 men, 18 of them old, because many of the adults had been away from camp hunting. They also counted the corpses of 90 women and 50 children. Major Baker accepted the number of deaths as 173, but he claimed to have killed 120 warriors in the attack.[28] Years later Bear Head described the villagers as having been on the verge of starvation. The buffalo had moved so far away that it took the hunters two or three days to find them. As they mourned the destruction, Black Antelope, one of the surviving old men wailed: "Why, oh why had it to be that all of our warriors, our hunters, had to go out for buffalo at this time. But for that some of the white seizers [soldiers] would also be lying here in death."[29]

Baker's report of having killed 120 grossly overestimated the number of Indian men killed. The two camps under attack included only 30 to

37 lodges. The figures varied depending on whether they included the nearby small camps that were not attacked. Estimates at the time suggest that each lodge rarely included more than 2 adult males. With some of them away hunting, there could have been few more than half of the 120 men that Baker reported to have killed. The death toll of 33 men that the Indians claimed, when added to those away from the village hunting, is far more believable than Baker's figure. If we discount the Piegan claims that many men were away hunting because of the below-zero temperatures and that 120 warriors died defending their lodges and families that morning, why did the attacking troops suffer only a single fatality and no men wounded? Surely, even if only motivated by their survival instinct, 120 men defending themselves would have inflicted more than a single fatality on the attackers. It is just beyond belief that the soldiers could have killed 120 Indian men and lose only 1 of their own men. In all history the U.S. Army has never been that good or the Indians that bad.

Whatever the actual number of men, women, and children who died at the Marias, news of the battle led to bitter debate over the incident and government dealings with the Indians. The results delighted General Sheridan, who had ordered Major Baker to "strike them hard." He wrote to Sherman that "I have the honor to report the complete success of an expedition sent against them . . . [and] I think this will end Indian troubles in Montana."[30] He guessed right. The Marias Massacre persuaded the Blackfeet to end their attacks on Americans, delighting many westerners. Area newspapers hailed Backer's attack as a great victory. Almost universally describing Indians as brutal savages who deserved to be destroyed, they cheered that Malcolm Clarke's murder had been avenged. The *Owylee Avalanche* in nearby Idaho Territory expressed the feelings of many pioneers. After praising the attack, it encouraged the soldiers to "[k]ill and roast [the Indians] as they do the pale face. Kill the squaws so the accursed race may cease to propagate. Kill the papooses."[31]

News of Baker's attack on the Piegans had the opposite effect in the East. There humanitarians and reformers denounced it. Less than two weeks after the fight Lieutenant William B. Pease, the Blackfeet agent, submitted the number of Indian deaths as only 33 men in addition to the 90 women and 50 children in Baker's account. Pease sent these figures to Colonel Sully, who forwarded them to commissioner of Indian Affairs, Eli Parker. They quickly became public when Vincent Colyer, secretary of the new Board of Indian Commissioners, whom westerners derided as "Vincent the Good," read some of Pease's letter at a House of Representatives hearing. He charged that the troops had killed only 15 adult men but at the same time slaughtered 50 children. His testimony brought blistering attacks on the army's tactics from the *New York Times* and *Harpers' Weekly*, which portrayed the fight on the Marias as just another example in "our Indian policy of extermination."[32]

Generals Sherman and Sheridan had faced similar criticism after Colonel George Custer's attack on Black Kettle's village on the Washita two years earlier. In fact, when he got Sheridan's enthusiastic report of the battle, Sherman urged his subordinate to "look out for the cries of those who think the Indians are so harmless, and obtain all possible evidence concerning the murders charged on them." Once slavery had been abolished, several prominent humanitarians turned their attention to Indian affairs and jumped into the fray, attacking Sheridan. Boston abolitionist Wendell Phillips described Sheridan's hands as "foul with Indian blood." William Lloyd Garrison denounced the general a having a "terrible invectiveness" of spirit toward the Indians. Lydia Child joined the chorus, berating Sheridan: his "approved method of teaching red men not to commit murder is to slaughter their wives and children!"[33]

At least three results followed the uproar over Baker's attack on the Marias. The first basically ended the major's chances for advancement in the army. Despite Sheridan's strong support, for the rest of his career he became known as Marias Baker. More troubling, news of the Marias attack reached Washington as Congress was debating the contentious issue of transferring oversight of Indian Affairs from the Department of the Interior back to the War Department, where it had been until 1849. In theory that would have replaced the existing confusion between civilians in charge of managing Indian Affairs and the army responsible for keeping peace in the West. Prior to the Marias incident it appeared that the transfer to the War Department had plenty of support in Congress, but the dispute over Baker's attack persuaded some congressmen to oppose the measure. In the move to reduce army influence over Indian policy, Congress also ended the practice of having regular army officers serve as Indian agents. We may question whether these moves made any difference in dealing with the western tribes in the decades that followed. The only certainty was that the Marias Massacre brought an uneasy peace to Montana.

CHAPTER 8

Skeleton Cave, 1872

On June 19 a hot and tired Colonel George Crook reached his new assignment: Tucson, the capital of Arizona Territory. With the temperature at 103 degrees he might have agreed with another traveler, who described the desert outpost as "a city of mud-boxes, dingy and dilapidated . . . littered with broken corrals, sheds, bake-ovens, carcasses of dead animals . . . parched naked and grimly desolate."[1] On his first day in town he met Governor Anson Stafford, who described the repeated and gory Apache raids that terrorized whites and other Indians in the territory. That same day Crook ordered all army officers in southern Arizona to send him whatever information they had that might help him plan his upcoming campaign against the Apaches.

As the reports trickled in, they depicted a grim situation. No group had escaped repeated Apache violence. As a result the invading Anglo-Americans, long-resident Mexicans, and native Indians all hated the seminomadic raiders. When invading whites entered Arizona, they became tangled in a confusing and dangerous situation. The Apache people they met had migrated into the area hundreds of years earlier. Like the previously discussed Sioux, Cheyenne, and Blackfeet peoples, they never had an overall tribal unity. Living in an area from Texas west to Arizona and south into northern Mexico, they included people now called Jicarillas, Lipans, Kiowa Apaches, Mescaleros, Western Apaches,

Chiricahuas, and the related Navajos. Each of these groups included smaller bands, some with only a few families. The larger bands usually followed respected chiefs. All of the Apaches shared closely related languages and social customs. Because other Indian people occupied much of the most fertile land by the time these newcomers moved into the Southwest, the Apaches occupied harsh desert or mountain areas, which forced them to settle in small groups to survive in the area.[2]

There the Apaches either continued earlier raiding practices or developed new ones. When the Spanish edged into the area, they offered the raiders one more target. The Europeans fought, traded with, and tried to incorporate the indigenous people into their system but failed repeatedly. After Mexico won its independence, Mexican authorities exchanged food and other supplies for peace. But their effort collapsed, as raids, kidnapping, and murder occurred. Occasionally negotiators reached ceasefire agreements, but all of those collapsed and violence continued. When the United States acquired the region, the tribesmen learned that the new international border offered them both opportunity and refuge: they raided in each country. With the 1853 Gadsden Purchase of southern Arizona from Mexico, the United States acquired nearly all of the dangerous Apache country. In much of the West Indian raiding represented only a hazardous supplement to the economy. In Arizona, by contrast, the harshness of the region and its limited resources meant that survival depended on raiding.[3]

Just a few years after the United States acquired southern Arizona, Apaches began raiding the newly arriving American pioneers. On January 27, 1861, two small parties of Indians attacked John Ward's small ranch, driving off twenty head of cattle and kidnapping his twelve-year-old stepson, Felix. The next morning Lieutenant George Bascom began to investigate. He found a few tracks that pointed east to the home territory of the Chiricahuas, who lived in southeast Arizona and southwest New Mexico. Although those Apaches had no history of taking prisoners, the settlers blamed the kidnapping on the band led by Cochise. Two days after the raid Lieutenant Bascom led fifty-four mounted infantrymen to Apache Pass in the heart of Chiricahua country. Once there he invited Cochise to meet for a council. Soldiers had passed through the area without any incidents, so the chief assumed that the parley presented no danger.[4]

On February 4, 1861, Bascom met the chief for lunch in his tent. There he accused Cochise's people of raiding Ward's ranch and kidnapping the boy. The chief denied the charge and offered to send runners to other bands that he thought might be holding young Felix. When he explained that it might take a week to ten days after finding the boy to have him returned, Bascom told his guest that he could leave but his companions would be held as hostages until the Indians returned Felix. Thinking that Bascom meant to seize him, Cochise slashed open the tent side with his knife and ran out of the camp before the astonished soldiers knew what had happened. During the next several days, the Apaches captured several whites. Cochise and Bascom exchanged messages over exchanging prisoners. On February 9 Cochise decided that Bascom had no intention of exchanging prisoners and ordered the captives killed. In retaliation Bascom had his men hang their Apache prisoners. That exchange, often called the "Bascom Affair," started a war with the Chiricahuas that lasted for another decade, spreading repeated violence and destruction across southern Arizona.[5]

The repeated Apache robberies, kidnappings, and murders infuriated their neighbors, who universally hated them. That hatred led directly to the April 30, 1871, Camp Grant Massacre of an entire Apache village. Two days earlier an armed mob of 6 Anglo-Americans, 48 Mexican Americans, and 92 Tohono O'odham men had ridden out of Tucson, looking for Apaches to kill. At Camp Grant Lieutenant Royal Whitman had persuaded nearly 500 Aravaipa and Pinal Apaches to settle nearby. Treated peacefully, they agreed to stop raiding and began cutting hay and wood for the post and nearby ranchers. Not aware of the approaching Tucson murderers, most of the men left their village to hunt. Early on April 30, while they combed the nearby mountains for game, disaster struck. The attackers raced into the undefended village, killing everyone they saw. They shot, stabbed, or clubbed 144 people to death. All but 8 of those were women and children. The victors later sold the 27 children who survived into slavery.[6]

When accounts of the slaughter reached the East, President Grant ordered that the attackers be arrested and tried. In September 1871 the U.S. district attorney, W. C. Rowell, charged with overseeing the case, reached Tucson and empaneled a grand jury to investigate the event. When local jurors refused to indict leaders of the raid, Rowell threatened that President Grant would declare martial law if they failed to do so and would have them tried by military courts-martial, far more threatening than a civil trial.[7] The jurors reluctantly gave the prosecutor the indictments that he demanded and charged 108 men with murder. When the townspeople learned this, an angry crowd burned effigies of Rowell and his clerk. Moving to protect them from mob violence, the commander at nearby Camp Lowell dispatched soldiers to the scene. During the five-day trial, the defense attorney admitted the attack but justified it by pointing to items found at the scene reportedly stolen in earlier raids. Nineteen minutes after the judge finished his charge, the jury found all of the defendants not guilty.[8]

There is no clear evidence that the Camp Grant Massacre persuaded President Grant to replace Colonel George Stoneman. The colonel had moved from Arizona to California, and local residents accused him of not fighting the Apaches vigorously enough. When his superiors first suggested that Lieutenant Colonel George Crook move south and take charge in Arizona, he had protested that he "was tired of the Indian work . . . [because] it only entailed hard work without any corresponding benefits."[9] Despite his objections Grant ordered that Crook be elevated to his brevet rank of colonel and be given command of the territory's defenses. Anything but a choice assignment, southern Arizona presented all the delights of the Sonoran Desert. Often the plants sported more thorns than leaves, while rattlesnakes, gila monsters, scorpions, and tarantulas awaited the unwary. One visitor commented that "hostility appeared to be the normal condition of everybody and everything" in the territory. General Sherman echoed this view: "we had one war with Mexico to take Arizona, and we should have another to make her take it back."[10]

Whatever his misgivings about being chosen to lead the Apache campaign ahead of several dozen colonels, George Crook quickly put his skills to work. Having asked his subordinate officers to send him information about the region and the Apaches, he poured over their responses, extracting descriptions of available trails, fords across existing streams, and even the quality of grass needed as forage for horses and mules.[11] He spent most of the summer preparing a campaign against the Apaches. When the governor and several other local leaders recommended using Mexicans as scouts because they knew the country, he enlisted fifty Mexicans as scouts. Unlike Colonel Stoneman, who rode a desk in California, on July 11, 1871, traveling on a mule, Crook led five companies of cavalry and his Destroying Angels, as he called the Mexican guides, across the desert east to Fort Bowie in the heart of Chiricahua territory. Along the march the troopers saw several small groups of Indians, but they rode away quickly.

After only a few days Crook realized that his Mexican scouts knew little about the country, so he decided to get other help and turned to recruiting Apaches. From Fort Bowie the troops rode north to Camp Grant. There he held long discussions with peaceful Apache leaders and recruited some of their men as scouts, promising them the same pay and equipment that the soldiers received. From there he led the column farther north to Camp Verde. Their successful mission took the colonel's men through the heart of Apache country, showing any doubtful band leaders the Americans' ability to reach their home villages or rancherias. When the column reached Camp Verde, Crook learned that news of the Camp Grant Massacre had so enraged the president that he had agreed to send the Board of Indian Commissioners secretary, Vincent Colyer, to pacify the Apaches with gifts rather than bullets. Disappointed at having to call off his planned thrust into Indian country, Crook saw this as an effort to "interfere with my operations"; having received orders to assist Colyer, however, the colonel halted his first Apache campaign.[12]

The commissioner had been in Arizona two years earlier and had created several new Apache reservations. Now armed with $70,000 that Congress had appropriated he returned with a directive "to take such actions as in your judgement [are best for] . . . locating the nomadic tribes of those Territories upon suitable reservations, bringing them under the control of the proper officers of the Indian department and supplying them with necessary subsistence and clothing."[13] Colyer met several groups of Apaches and persuaded them to accept reservations near existing military posts. He assured them that if they remained peaceful the soldiers would protect rather than attack them and promised food and other material. Without any long tradition of raising their own crops, farming, always difficult in the desert Southwest, had attracted few of the Indians. Colyer explained that "danger from the whites, ineffective arms for the chase and a scarcity of game" explained Apache raiding. When their white visitor now promised food if they remained peaceful, he reported that many band leaders accepted his offer.[14] In response the secretary of the interior, Columbus Delano, ordered that the Indians be moved to the reservations for protection and feeding.

As the Indians moved to these reservations, white Arizonians objected bitterly. Ridiculing him as "Vincent the Good," they denounced Colyer's view that Anglo-Americans had caused the violence by mistreatment of the Apaches and that the Indians only wanted to be left alone. John Marion, editor of the *Prescott Miner*, echoed their views, labeling the visiting peacemaker as a "cold blooded scoundrel," a "red-handed assassin," and a "black-hearted dog."[15] Crook treated his visitor cordially even though they disagreed fundamentally about how to deal with the Apaches. No Indian hater, the colonel shared the views of most senior army commanders. Peaceful Indians deserved fair treatment, but those choosing hostilities needed to be defeated and pushed onto reservations. He doubted that Colyer's actions would bring lasting peace. Once "Vincent the Good" left the territory, the colonel returned to reorganizing his aborted expedition against the Apaches.

Highly competent and a stickler for detail, Crook oversaw every aspect of the preparations. Fully persuaded that only other Apaches would be able to track and capture the hostile Indians, during autumn 1871 he recruited scouts from many groups. As strange as it seems today, the various bands felt no allegiance to each other and in fact sometimes fought each other. For many young Apache men joining the soldiers' campaigns had several attractions. First, it allowed them to hone their skills as trackers and warriors. They also received weapons, ammunition, food, and the same pay as the soldiers did when they agreed to join Crook's forays. These inducements helped the colonel recruit scouts whose knowledge helped him to force most of the Apaches onto reservations.

Having secured men who knew the country and the locations of hostile groups, Crook turned his attention to the crucial matter of transporting food and ammunition for his men. He recognized that the rugged terrain made using wagons to carry supplies and equipment, as was done in the campaigns on the plains, only a recipe for disaster. He chose to use pack trains instead. Crook considered the existing contracting system that supplied the troops undependable and a source of corruption. So instead of using the local contractors, he hired the most skilled packers to manage his supply columns. Preferring mules to horses because they were stronger, more surefooted, and smarter, he spent days choosing sturdy pack animals with healthy hooves. Having identified them, he designed new pack cushions and picked well-fitting saddles for the mules. As one of his aides reported, "Every article used in these pack-trains had to be of the best materials [because] . . . it was impossible to replace anything broken, and a column might be embarrassed by the failure of a train to arrive with ammunition or rations."[16]

On November 21, 1871, General John Schofield issued orders to Crook that specified how he was to deal with the Arizona Indians: all Indian bands in Arizona had to move onto one of the newly created reservations. Any who refused would be considered hostile. The general directed that army officers serve as agents at each reservation. They were to keep lists of all adult males, issue identification to each, and take roll each day to ensure that they had not left to raid.[17] Colonel Crook echoed Schofield's directive, and in December 1871 he sent word to the bands that they had to move to the reservations that Colyer had set up or be considered hostile.

When almost no more Apache bands responded to his ultimatum, Crook worked to renew the campaign that he had aborted some months earlier. He was confident that he had prepared his men and equipment effectively. Then news of a new massacre of whites near Wickenburg reached him. On November 5 Indians attacked a stagecoach and killed six of the eight passengers. One of the victims, Frederick W. Loring, had been a correspondent attached to Lieutenant George Wheeler's expedition along the Colorado River. He was a well-connected Boston journalist, so his death received wide attention in the Northeast. Local evidence suggested that the Yavapai Apaches had committed the raid, and Crook's inquiry brought the same result. The evidence pointed to the Date Creek Yavapais as the guilty band.[18]

As Crook prepared to restart his campaign in response to this new attack, and almost before the dust from Colyer's visit could settle, news came from Washington that the president had sent General Oliver O. Howard to continue the peace initiative that the commissioner had begun. In 1862 Howard had lost an arm in Civil War fighting. Three years later he became head of the newly created Freedmen's Bureau to help former slaves. A self-righteous, Bible-thumping man, Howard rarely took advice. Even the diplomatic Crook had some trouble dealing with the so-called praying general. The colonel reported being amused by

Howard's idea that God had appointed him to "be Moses to the Negro . . . and that his next mission was with the Indian."[19] Despite their tensions Howard and Crook worked together without any major disputes.

With Crook's second effort to march into Apache country halted, Howard send messengers to Cochise inviting him to a meeting to end the fighting. The general's instructions called for him to negotiate peace with the Apache leader. Once he had done that he was "to induce them [the Apaches] to abandon their present habits of life and go upon permanent reservations." When the Chiricahua leader refused to meet him, Howard took several Western Apache chiefs to Washington to meet officials there. Then he returned to Arizona, recruited Tom Jeffords, whom Cochise trusted, to lead him to the chief, and traveled into the Chiricahua homeland. When Howard declared that he came looking for peace, the chief responded that "nobody wants peace more than I do." The two negotiators had to wait several weeks for the other Chiricahua chiefs to arrive, but when they did Howard and Cochise agreed to a peace treaty. The general promised a new reservation in southeastern Arizona, and the chief demanded that Tom Jeffords be appointed as the new agent.[20]

Although the new agreement related only to the Chiricahuas and failed to stop the continued raiding by the Western Apache bands in central Arizona, it meant that Crook could focus his efforts on them rather than on all the Apaches. In fact, repeated Yavapai attacks on whites since Colyer had erroneously proclaimed that he had achieved peace had resulted in the deaths of three soldiers and forty-one civilians.[21] Even before having to suspend his campaign a second time because of General Howard's arrival in Arizona, Crook had proclaimed that after February 15, 1872, "all Apache Indians found outside of these Reservations, will be considered and treated as hostile."[22] Wisely, the colonel sent messages to each band and the larger rancherias, sometimes using spies or allowing detainees to escape and spread the news. This helped him avoid the situation faced earlier by Colorado governor Evans, when the Cheyenne bands out on the plains hunting never got his message to return to their reservation in the Sand Creek disaster.

When few of the missing Apaches appeared at the reservations, Crook began his campaign. Like other commanders fighting Indians on the plains, he chose winter as the best time to attack. He expected his troops to find the scattered rancherias, drive the Indians from their secluded camps, capture or kill some of them, and destroy their shelters, clothing, and food supplies. If done right, that would leave the Indians scattered, short of food, and worried about more fighting. Once the troops found and destroyed some of the camps, Crook expected his men to drive the Apaches into an ever-shrinking area, where the winter weather, food shortages, and continuing fighting would force the survivors onto the reservations.

For the campaign Crook divided his mixed force of infantry, cavalry, Indian scouts, and mule train packers into nine nearly independent highly mobile units that he called "expeditions." While each of these included experienced Indian fighters, all of them depended heavily on the skills of their thirty to a hundred Indian scouts. These men knew the country as well as the fugitives' likely camping places and proved crucial for the campaign's success. At the beginning of the campaign men from several tribes served as scouts, but by the end they were mostly Apaches. The columns crisscrossed the Yavapai homeland from all directions to convince them that there was no escape from the soldiers. Before sending the units out, the colonel told them to allow those who wanted to surrender to do so. But if "they prefer to fight, they were to get all the fighting they wanted. . . . In either case [they] were to be hunted down until the last [one] is killed or captured." He ordered them to avoid killing women or children and abusing any of their prisoners. Once the shooting ended, he told them to enlist prisoners as scouts whenever possible, because they would best knew the hiding places of those still out.[23]

Winter in the Tonto Basin and the nearby high country brought zero temperatures and often high snow to the region. That usually encouraged the Yavapais to move down into the lower valleys, but with Crook's highly mobile columns moving through the region the fugitives had to stay in the mountains. Often they went without fires to escape detection and had less game available than in the valleys. Some of the scouts knew where particular groups had their food stored for winter, and the troops destroyed those supplies whenever they found them. Individual patrols tracked, met, and fought the hostiles in repeated small-scale fights, from which the Apaches "fled, leaving everything behind." By early December 1872 Crook's aide, Lieutenant John Bourke, expected the campaign to succeed: as he noted, "these incorrigible devils . . . are without an article of clothing, a particle of food, or any necessaries."[24]

On December 27, 1872, the troops found a Yavapai rancheria when a six-year-old Apache boy told them about a large cave in the cliff along the Salt River. That night the soldiers learned that their scouts had seen campfires in the canyon below and rested uneasily, waiting for morning. Early the next day a handful of men made their way down a steep trail, where they found a small abandoned camp, a herd of horses, and then a well-protected rancheria in "an almost impregnable position." Lieutenant William Ross reported seeing a large cave with several men dancing in front of the fire and women preparing food next to them. He ordered his men to open fire: they killed six of the dancers. Caught totally by surprise, the Indians failed to shoot back immediately. Their hesitation gave the rest of the troops time to race down the steep trail, form a firing line, and move into position blocking escape.[25]

Captain William Brown took charge. Realizing that the Apaches' location gave them no chance to escape, he offered them a chance to surrender. They responded with a "shriek of hatred and defiance . . . yells . . . that not one of us should ever see the light of another day but should furnish a banquet for the crows and buzzards."[26] Brown offered the Yavapais a second chance to surrender, but they responded with more jeers. Trying to follow his orders to spare the women and children, he proposed that they send the noncombatants to safety, but they responded that they intended to fight to the finish. The cave defenders sent flights of arrows over Brown's men like artillery fire, but they missed everyone. Inside the cave the defenders stood behind a ten-foot-high rock wall and exchanged fire with soldiers equally protected by rock outcroppings.

Seeing no other way to shoot the well-protected defenders, Captain Brown ordered his men to fire up at the cave roof. This caused many of the bullets to ricochet downward, striking people in the cave. Some of the shots also showered the defenders with rock shards, which may have caused as many wounds as the gunfire. Soon the soldiers heard the cries of wounded women and children. Another group of whites began firing down into the cave from above. When firing from the cave continued, the attackers above the cave began dropping boulders on the defenders. By noon the shooting had ended. Brown's men entered the cave, now littered with dead and wounded. Fifty-seven of the Indians had died in the battle, and the troops took thirty-five women and children prisoners.

Many of the captives had been wounded, and only twenty survived. The victors suffered only one fatality, a Pima scout. After working their way through the cave and destroying the food and other items littering the floor, the troops left the dead where they fell. Their bleached bones gave the cavern its modern name: Skeleton Cave.[27]

Brown's column had destroyed the band hidden in the cave. But Apache society contained many small bands, so the troops had to continue finding and attacking other rancherias. By late March 1873 the attacking columns had found most of the hostile camps. The last major battle at took place at Turret Mountain along the Verde River, where Captain George Randall's force captured an Apache woman. They persuaded her to guide them to a major rancheria, which they attacked at dawn. The Indians had felt so secure that fire from Randall's men spread panic in the camp. Rather than staying to fight, the men broke and fled. Some of them ran directly in front of the troops, who shot them down quickly. Others escaped by fleeing down the steep cliffs. The troops captured only women and children. This victory broke nearly all Apache resistance and ended the threat of widespread Indian raids.[28]

Several weeks later Crook reported that large numbers of Apaches had come in with "the most abject pleas for peace . . . [I] have concluded a peace with them that I believe will be lasting."[29] Writing to show how thoroughly he had defeated the Indians, he described the captives as "emaciated [with] clothes torn in tatters, some of their legs not thicker than my arms."[30] Apache leaders admitted that the whites' firepower and use of Indian scouts had defeated them. Old Chalipun told the colonel: "You see, we're [sic] are nearly dead from want of food and exposure." And Old Deltchay, whom the troops called "The Liar," confessed that his band had shrunk from 125 men to a mere 20 when the fighting ended. The whites' pursuit of his band succeeded so well that "they could get no sleep at nights" and jumped up at every sound, fearing that the soldiers had found them.[31]

Gradually Indians and whites alike came to call the December fight on the Salt River the Skeleton Cave Massacre. Some might say that, like the Seventh Cavalry attack on Black Kettle's village on the Washita, this incident should be called a battle rather than a massacre. The result of the frontier army's practice of total war brought death to the elderly, women, and children as well as to the men who actually did the fighting. Unlike earlier battles in this study, here the troops offered a chance for surrender and safety rather than destruction, but the Apache leaders rejected that option, dooming nearly all those caught in the cave that morning to death or injury.

CHAPTER 9

Fort Robinson, 1878–1879

The 1879 destruction of Dull Knife's band of Northern Cheyennes differed from the other events discussed here. Unlike the rest of these encounters, no U.S. troops launched an unsuspected dawn attack on a sleeping village. Nor had the Indians fought against the United States just before the event. They had fled from the Southern Cheyenne home at the Darlington Agency in Indian Territory. Their effort to escape near-starvation and disease and return to their former home in eastern Montana led to disaster. When overtaken by troops, some of them agreed to move to Fort Robinson in northwestern Nebraska. There they learned that U.S. authorities still demanded that they return south so that all parts of the tribe would be at the same place. They refused. After suffering inhumane treatment meant to force them to go south, they tried to escape. The pursuing troops killed many of them.

As noted earlier, by the mid-nineteenth century the Cheyenne people had divided into three distinct groups. The northern Cheyenne bands lived and hunted in a vast area extending from south of the Platte River north to Montana. They joined their Sioux neighbors in joint buffalo hunts and raids on the Pawnees or Crows, even sharing camps and villages with them. Few white intruders except the fur traders and only a handful of government explorers disturbed their lives. Meanwhile, the Southern Cheyennes lived on the central plains in an area that stretched south from the Platte to the Arkansas River and beyond. They joined the neighboring Arapahos for their annual hunts. Their homeland had fewer buffalo. After the 1848 gold discovery in California, many more pioneers moved west through their territory than through the lands of the northern Cheyennes. The third tribal division included several semi-independent military societies called the Dog Soldiers, who lived and hunted between the northern and southern bands. These groups attracted mostly young warriors and hunters, who looked for excitement and rejected the advice and leadership of the traditional chiefs. As seen in the earlier events at Sand Creek and the Washita, the three divisions in Cheyenne society complicated relations with the expanding frontier population and government officers responsible for keeping peace. The whites considered the Cheyennes a single united tribe even though few of the Indians accepted that idea.

The Pike's Peak gold rush between 1858 and 1861 brought tens of thousands of white miners into the Southern Cheyenne homeland and helped persuade their chiefs to sign the 1861 Treaty of Fort Wise. That agreement surrendered 90 percent of the tribe's land and committed the Southern Cheyennes to move onto land lacking buffalo for hunting or water for farming. It also reduced connections between the northern and southern bands to little more than wishful thinking. By the time of the 1864 Sand Creek Massacre of Black Kettle's band by Colorado militiamen, each band considered itself independent from the others. While the region between the two areas included valuable hunting lands, few but members of the warrior societies traveled through it to pursue buffalo.[1]

While Southern Cheyennes surrendered most of their territory to American negotiators, their northern relatives became close allies of the Sioux and claimed land along what became the Bozeman Trail in Wyoming. In July 1866 they met Colonel Henry Carrington at the newly created Fort Reno. The chiefs objected to the Americans coming into their country and warned Carrington not to build any more forts in the region. In a blunt confrontation they asked: "What are you doing in this country anyhow?" Before he could answer, they charged: "You come here and kill our game; you cut our grass and chop down our trees; you break our rocks [mine], and you kill our people. This country belongs to us, and we want you to get out of it."[2] Either Carrington failed to alert his superiors or they ignored his messages, because troops soon built Fort Phil Kearny and began work on a third new post that became Fort C. F. Smith to protect the Bozeman Trail, right in the middle of the Sioux and Cheyenne prime buffalo-hunting area.

The new forts and continuing traffic on the Bozeman Trail supplying the miners in Montana strengthened the ties between the Northern Cheyenne and Sioux tribes. Soon warriors from both groups began harassing troops along the trail. In mid-October and early December 1866 the Indians attacked small wood-gathering parties near Fort Kearny, killing several men and evading the troops. After several minor raids on wood-cutting detachments, on December 21, 1866, reports of a large Indian raiding party persuaded Carrington to dispatch Captain William Fetterman with a force of seventy-six soldiers, three officers, and two civilians to counter the raiders. The commander warned Fetterman not to pursue any Indians who seemed to be fleeing, but the captain ignored his orders and marched into an ambush, losing his entire command. Two years later General William T. Sherman led the Indian Peace Commission in talks with the tribes on the northern plains. During the negotiations Northern Cheyenne leaders agreed to leave the area and join the Crows in Montana, the Sioux in South Dakota, or their cousins in Indian Territory within a year.[3]

Rather than moving, the Indians remained on the northern plains. In the autumn of 1870 a new U.S. Indian Commission met the Cheyennes at Fort Laramie. The chiefs told the visitors that they had no interest in joining their Southern Cheyenne relatives in Indian Territory. They insisted that the northern plains was their home and criticized the commissioners, saying that "the white man that came to make [the earlier] treaties told untruths."[4] By 1872 the government had attached the Northern Cheyennes to the Red Cloud Agency in northwestern Nebraska, but federal officials still wanted to locate all of the Cheyennes in one place. They accomplished that in 1873 when they invited chiefs from both the northern and southern bands to Washington, D.C., for a conference. The commissioner of Indian Affairs, E. P. Smith, insisted that neither the Crows nor the Sioux wanted to share their land with the Northern Cheyennes, so under the terms of the 1868 treaty they had to move south to Indian Territory. President Ulysses S. Grant met his visitors and repeated what the commissioner had told them. When the chiefs continued to balk, Congress stepped in to settle the dispute. The 1874 act appropriating funds for Indian Affairs withheld tribal annuity funds from both the Northern Cheyennes and Arapahos until they agreed to move south.[5]

Apparently hunting on the northern plains gave the Cheyennes enough food and buffalo robes for trade, because they ignored the new demand that they leave the northern plains. In fact, in the summer of 1876 chiefs Dull Knife and Little Wolf joined their Sioux allies to fight against U.S. troops and took part in the destruction of George Armstrong Custer and most of the Seventh Cavalry at the Battle of the Little Bighorn that June. Stung by biting criticism, the army began a determined hunt for Sioux and Cheyenne bands across the northern plains that fall and conducted a winter campaign against them. On November 25 of that year troops led by Colonel Ranald Mackenzie found Cheyenne chief Dull Knife's village on the Powder River in Montana Territory. Camp leaders knew that the soldiers had moved close but refused to take the threat seriously. When the soldiers stormed into the village, they caught most of the people sleeping. The troops scattered the Indians, captured many of their horses, and burned the lodges as well as the collected food, clothing, equipment, and weapons that the people had gathered for the winter. A lieutenant remembered that the villagers had 205 canvas lodges, which the Indian Department had given them. One of the surviving Cheyenne women acknowledged the destruction. In its aftermath she described the villagers as struggling through the snow: "Most of us were afoot. We had no lodges, only a few blankets, and there was only a little dried meat food among us. Men died of [their] wounds, women and children froze to death."[6]

The survivors joined a multiband camp led by Dull Knife, Little Wolf, and several other chiefs. Continuing the winter campaign in January 1877, General Nelson Miles attacked this village too. This convinced some of the Cheyennes to surrender, but most of them joined Crazy Horse and his Sioux followers. At first their hosts treated them well. As more Cheyennes straggled into the crowded camp, however, Crazy Horse became less generous. As the winter wore on, relations with their Oglala allies deteriorated. Cheyenne leaders decided that they had to surrender. In April Little Wolf rode into the Red Cloud Agency in northwestern Nebraska, leading 1,400 Cheyennes, to meet the soldiers. There General George Crook moved quickly to enlist some of the men in the army. They joined his force of 200 Sioux, Cheyenne, and Arapaho scouts who would campaign alongside the troops. Two weeks later, on April 21, Dull Knife and Standing Elk rode to the agency to surrender. The Indians had suffered from lack of food, clothing, and shelter since Mackenzie's attack nearly five months earlier. Many families had no blankets or cooking utensils, and most of the people were barefoot. Crook gave them time to settle in and offered food and medical treatment to the visitors. His straightforward manner convinced the chiefs that they could trust him. The council the next day ended with apparent harmony.[7]

Unfortunately for the Indians, the soldiers could only recommend how the tribal people should be treated. No matter what the officers seemed to promise, the commissioner of Indian Affairs and other federal officials had the final say. They remained determined to combine Northern Cheyennes and Southern Cheyennes in Indian Territory. Whether the chiefs knew it or not, a newspaper correspondent reported that a few Indians, led by Standing Elk, favored the idea, despite the Cheyenne leaders' opposition. They had relatives among the Southern Cheyennes and agreed to accept the move. One of the other chiefs charged that the officers at the agency gave Standing Elk more presents than the others in order to get his support. Divisions among the Indians weakened their resolve, but Colonel Mackenzie ignored their wishes even when they continued to speak against the move. Instead he lied, claiming that the 1,400 Cheyennes "desire to go to the southern agency at Fort Reno, on the Canadian River, Indian Territory."[8]

Once the arguing stopped, the people prepared to move south. On May 28, 1877, Lieutenant Henry Lawton organized their march. He reported that 972 Cheyennes who began the trek planned to follow old routes that the Indians had traveled when visiting friends and family decades earlier. The column of wagons and riders stretched for nearly two miles, with Fourth Regiment cavalrymen leading the way as they departed from the Red Cloud Agency. Thirty Cheyenne scouts escorted the migrants, riding along the flanks of the column. Most people walked, but the elderly and sick rode in the supply wagons. The Indians' pony herd and some beef cattle to feed the people on their march followed. After the first day most of the cavalrymen returned to Camp Robinson. Lieutenant Lawton had only fifteen troopers left to direct his charges. He used the Indian scouts to find good camping places with enough grass and water for the animals and to hunt for game to assure a fresh supply of meat. The wagons also carried bread, coffee, sugar, and other food for the trip. The travelers moved south across western Kansas and then east to present Dodge City. They stopped at Fort Dodge to receive rations and then moved on to Camp Supply in Oklahoma. On August 5, 1877, after seventy days of travel, they came to Fort Reno, just across the river from their new home at the Darlington Agency.[9]

Although the travelers appeared to have enjoyed their trip and the good hunting along the way, the scene in Indian Territory disappointed them. The flat, grass-covered countryside lacked the pine-covered hills that they had just left. Yet Old Whirlwind, a chief who had invited them to come south when the chiefs had visited Washington earlier, welcomed them. "Brothers," he told them, "we are very happy that you have come down and joined us. We are glad you have come to make this your country, to live with us as one people."[10] Despite his friendly reception, some followers of Dull Knife, Little Wolf, and Wild Hog complained that the agency Indians had failed to welcome them properly. This just was not true. The southerners gave the newcomers food and other needed items, held feasts in their honor, and did their best to help them all get settled. Most of the northerners, but not all, accepted the help and ceremonies gladly.

Perhaps some of them had expected more elaborate feasts or something else to acknowledge their arrival. Whatever the reasons, more than three hundred of the northerners decided to live apart from those already at the agency and camped about five miles from its headquarters. They complained repeatedly that their new home had little in common with the region they had just left. High temperatures, ticks, mosquitoes, and horseflies all bothered them. They found few trees or bushes with nuts or fruit, and the buffalo and other big game animals had all been killed. Colonel Mackenzie, who had helped to supervise their deportation from Nebraska, arrived at Fort Reno soon after they arrived. He ordered a tribal census and then seized their horse herd, allowing just one pony for each lodge. The others he ordered sold. The money was used to buy cattle so that the newcomers could begin raising their own livestock. That made sense on the plains, but the Indians had so little food that they quickly killed the animals to feed themselves. Many of Mackenzie's actions ignored or overlooked provisions of the 1868 treaty, which had promised a good cow and a yoke of oxen for each lodge and daily rations of meat and flour. The agreement said nothing about their having to surrender their horses.[11]

Cultural differences between the northerners and southerners complicated agency life. About six hundred of the immigrants accepted their new situation, while just over three hundred remained aloof and dissatisfied. They quarreled with the agent over the way he gave out the rations. They criticized the southerners for having accepted some white customs and farming. The newcomers refused to send their children to school, plant crops, or spend time listening to Christian missionaries. When the schools beat Indian children for misbehaving, the newcomers asked their southern cousins: "Will you let the white wolf whip your boys?"[12] Having been exposed to these things for a generation or more, the southerners at least tolerated them. That led some of the northerners to taunt them for being afraid to resist the whites.

When urged to become farmers, the men objected. They considered farming to be women's work and degrading for warriors. Instead of taking up the plow, some bragged about having been at the Little Bighorn massacre of Custer. These disputes encouraged some of the newcomers to remain in the isolated camps and outside the routine agency activities. They also created growing frustration, anger, and nostalgia as well as a feeling that the whites had lied to them. Their disastrous 1877–78 winter buffalo hunt reinforced that belief. When white negotiators had told them that they had to move south, they had promised that there were plenty of buffalo there for them to hunt. That proved false. Instead Chief Wild Hog reported that they found so few buffalo during the hunt that "we had to kill a good many of our ponies to eat to save ourselves from starving." With disease, hunger, and homesickness as motivations, by the summer of 1878 the most conservative of the migrants had made up their minds that they could not survive another year in Indian Territory.[13]

They decided to leave the agency and return to their northern home. While meeting with their agent John Miles, Chief Little Wolf told him of their determination to leave Indian Territory. He reminded the agent that the Cheyennes thought Generals Crook and Mackenzie had promised that they could return to the North if the South was not satisfactory. He went on to contrast their life in the North with life at the Darlington Agency and asked for permission to return to their former homeland immediately. If Miles lacked the authority to let them move, Little Wolf asked for a chance to visit Washington and plead his case there. The agent replied that if his people stayed in Indian Territory for another year, he would consider their request. Chief Little Wolf objected: "No, we cannot stay another year; we want to go now." In another year "we may all be dead and there will be none of us left to travel north."[14] After this exchange the agent accused the chief of encouraging some of his band to flee the agency and travel north.

As soon as this contentious meeting ended, Cheyenne leaders began their plans for their flight north. They asked for two weeks' rations rather than one week's in order to start their trek with some food on hand. Some of the young men began stealing horses. On September 5, 1878, a delegation of their southern Cheyenne neighbors complained to agent Miles about the lost horses. They accused the northerners of having taken them. When the agent asked why they thought Indians taken the horses rather than white horse thieves, they answered quickly: "These thieves are particular. They take only a few good horses from a herd, always picking out the best. White men would just round up the whole bunch and run them off."[15] The planners also buried their weapons and ammunition to be certain that the troops would not find them.

As they prepared, the chiefs decided to move farther from the agency. That convinced agent Miles that they were about to flee. He asked officers at Fort Reno to send troops to keep an eye on the new camp. Having heard that some of Little Wolf's followers had already started north, he ordered them to return to the agency for a census, but few responded. On September 9 he sent for the chiefs to meet him. They argued heatedly. Miles claimed that three of the Cheyennes had started north and demanded that Little Wolf give him ten men as hostages until the troops could capture and return the runaways. The chief replied that the troops "could never get back these three, and you never would set my men free. You would keep them always." When the agent threatened to force the chief to give him the hostages, Little Wolf reminded him that during his visit to Washington the president had urged him to remain at peace. He ended with a warning to "listen to what I say to you. I am going to leave here; I am going to my own country. . . . If you are going to send your soldiers after me. . . . I will fight you."[16]

The dissidents prepared to flee from their hated agency on the evening of September 9. They sent boys with valuable goods to trade for ammunition, dug up their cached weapons, filled their pemmican bags, packed clothing and extra food, stole a few more horses, and took down their lodge covers. They left the lodge poles standing and the village fires burning, hoping to deceive the nearby troops into believing that all was well, and silently rode into the night. Following Dull Knife, Little Wolf, Hog, Tangle Hair, and Bull Hump, the 353 men, women, and children set out as a well-disciplined military movement. Scouts led the group. Men and a few of the women rode, while the other women and children walked. Some of the young men followed with the four or five hundred horses that they had gathered for the journey.[17]

The fugitives had barely started their flight when American Horse, one of the Northern Cheyenne chiefs who chose to remain at Darlington, reported their movement early the next morning. Captain Joseph Rendle-brock led two companies of the Fourth Cavalry from Fort Reno and some Indian scouts in pursuit. The captain had orders to trap the runaways at the flooding Arkansas River, but he hoped to overtake the Cheyennes with his 85-man column sooner. On September 13 he did so at Turkey Springs. Rendlebrock sent an Arapaho scout to ask the chiefs to surrender and return south to Darlington. The Indian men began to encircle the troops during this exchange, and Rendlebrock ordered his men to begin firing. The fighting lasted all day. During the night the Cheyenne fighters set fire to the grass around the cavalrymen's camp. Defeated, the soldiers retreated to safety, having done little damage to the Indians.[18]

For the next two weeks the fugitives moved north across Kansas, fighting defensive battles at Bluff Creek, Big Sandy, and Punished Woman's Fork along the way. The troops captured and destroyed the Cheyenne pony herd at the fork, severely limiting their mobility and food supply. This also persuaded some of the young fighting men that they needed to increase their raids on the whites they met if they were to get more animals and food for the more than three hundred people in their band. As they moved north, Cheyenne raiders stole cattle, horses, and mules from the ranches along the way. Although the chiefs urged the young men to avoid attacking the civilian population along their route, they ignored the warnings. On September 29 and October 3, 1878, they went on a rampage against the farm families that they met in Decatur and Rawlins Counties in northwest Kansas. They killed thirty-one people and raped at least ten women and girls, one only nine years old. The chiefs claimed that the raiders never told them what they had done because they knew that the leaders would disapprove. Their rampage in Kansas undercut what had become a growing sympathy for the migrants as well as fueling white hatred and calls for vengeance in the West.[19]

Fleeing from pursuing groups of townspeople, farmers, ranchers, and hunters, the Indians realized that they needed to avoid the soldiers approaching from nearly every direction. They rode northwest on newly stolen horses, crossing the Union Pacific tracks then a few days later the North Platte River before entering the Nebraska Sand Hills on their way to the Black Hills of western South Dakota. In early October Dull Knife and Little Wolf argued about where to go. Dull Knife and his followers wanted to join their relatives living with the Oglala Sioux at the Red Cloud Agency in Nebraska, but by then the government had closed the agency and moved the Sioux to the Pine Ridge Agency. Little Wolf wanted to continue northwest to Montana Territory, so the group divided. A few days later Dull Knife and nearly 150 others left the camp. His followers included mostly old men, women, and children, although Wild Hog and Tangle Hair stayed with the group. They had no realistic hope of joining the Sioux, because Red Cloud's people now served as scouts for the army, actively hunting the Cheyennes. On October 23 the refugees met the pursuing federal troops. The scouts persuaded them not to resist. The next morning they surrendered their horses and most of their weapons. On October 26, 1878, the army wagons brought the 46 men, 61 women, and 42 children into Fort Robinson. Their pilgrimage had ended.[20]

The Cheyennes moved into a long barracks building and had the freedom to move around the post. Major Caleb Carleton explained that they had to remain at the fort for three months while the government decided what to do with them. Then he warned them that "if one man of you deserts or runs away, you will not be treated like this any longer. You will be held responsible for him."[21] Carleton seemed friendly but placed guards both in and outside the building and ordered the barracks searched for weapons several times. Those efforts located only a few old weapons in addition to the twenty-five guns that the Cheyennes had surrendered earlier, and the major worried that his prisoners had more weapons. He was correct, but he had no idea that they had placed most of them and their bows underneath the barracks floor and that the women and children wore parts of other weapons attached to their clothes as decorations.[22]

For several weeks the Indians received good food at the post and new moccasins from the nearby Sioux. The post physician treated the sick and injured as they recovered from their travel. During the day the men smoked and played cards, but they never could leave the barracks area. The women could walk down to the river. In the evenings some of the young people held dances. Yet their fear that the government might try to send them back south kept many of them worried. Dull Knife and Wild Hog asked Carleton to move them to the Red Cloud Agency that had been closed. When he told them that he had no authority to do that, they insisted that they would never return south. Observers recognized the Cheyennes' refusal to return to Indian Territory, although federal officials ignored it. One newsman reported that "they will never return to the Indian Territory unless tied hand and foot and dragged there like dead cattle."[23]

The major had told the chiefs that none of the band could be away from the fort overnight. When Dull Knife's son Bull Hump left to visit his wife at the Pine Ridge Agency, the post commander ordered the prisoners to be locked in the barracks. In early December the government decided to return the Northern Cheyennes south to Indian Territory immediately. General George Crook, commanding the department, asked to delay the move until winter had ended, but his superiors refused. At the same time Captain Henry Wessells took command at Fort Robinson. He met with the prisoners, but his repeated efforts to persuade them to return to Darlington Agency failed. On January 5, 1879, he stopped feeding them and cut off their supply of wood to heat the barracks. Three days later he stopped giving them drinking water, and the guards refused to let the Indians out of the building to gather snow that they could melt for water. When those measures failed, Wessells applied more pressure. He took Wild Hog and Old Crow hostage. The soldiers let Wild Hog return to the barracks but kept him outside while he persuaded nineteen of the old and sick to leave the building.[24]

Assuming that they would die either on the winter trip south or from disease once they reached Indian Territory, the rest of the Cheyennes decided that they would try to escape. One of the leaders said: "We will not die shut up here like dogs; we will die on the prairie; we will die fighting."[25] On January 9 they tore up the barracks flooring, grabbed their bows, arrows, and guns, smashed open the windows, and shot the guards as they fled. The remaining guards began shooting, while the 125 Indians disappeared into the night. They ran toward the river with the troopers firing wildly and chasing them. A few of the men formed a rear guard and fought off the soldiers temporarily: all but one of them died in the fighting. The Cheyennes ran toward a nearby sawmill, while the troops poured fire on them. A visiting newsman reported that "their bleeding bodies mangled and torn . . . literally strewed the road."[26] In a fury the soldiers killed many of the wounded and committed other atrocities during the fighting. A local rancher who arrived that day wrote that "many of the dead were powder-burned" from close range executions.[27] A civilian employee at the fort saw two dead women with their dresses pulled up, raped with wooden stakes.[28]

When the shooting stopped the next day, 35 of the escapees had been recaptured; another 27 were dead. Farther from the fort the soldiers hunted others who had fled in small groups. Pursuing troops killed one small group of 5 women while they tried to shelter a few children. Determined to round up the remaining Cheyennes, Captain Wessells sent patrols through the hills to find them. Often they met small groups of 2 or 3 people who resisted and died or fled, only to have the soldiers track them down in a day or two. In several instances the soldiers shot weak or sick old men and women as well as any wounded teenaged boys they came across. At the same time, they also rescued abandoned babies and small children, bringing them to safety at the fort.[29]

During the pursuit a group of about 18 men and their families came together. Refusing to surrender, they fought and moved to fight again. After eluding the soldiers, their luck ended on January 22 when troops surrounded Little Finger Nail's party of 18 men and boys old enough to fight and 14 women and children. Three companies of soldiers (147 men and 5 officers) attacked the tired and freezing runaways hidden in what their attackers called the pit. After nearly an hour of vicious fighting, Captain Wessells called for a cease-fire and asked the Indians to surrender. Like the Yavapais at Skeleton Cave in Arizona, they replied with more shots. When the firing stopped, 23 Cheyennes had died in the pit. The next day 3 of the wounded died. Of the 147 Northern Cheyennes who had arrived at Camp Robinson months earlier, 107 took part in the attempted escape. In the days between their breakout on January 9 and

January 23, the soldiers killed 64 of the Cheyennes and captured another 68, while some others just disappeared.[30]

The Northern Cheyenne experience included no surprise attack on a resting village as so many other events discussed here did, but the stories have much in common. The forced move south into Indian Territory resulted from the refusal of U.S. officials to learn something about their charges or to listen to Indian leaders. The troubles at Darlington Agency grew out of the clumsy and ineffective contract supply system, which often provided spoiled food and rotten meat and gave the recipients food items totally unfamiliar to them. Indian Office rules allowing the local agent to withhold promised treaty items did little to ease discontent. The lack of medical attention and the unavailability of necessary medicines only made matters worse. Other indigenous groups faced similar challenges, such as forced removal, but few exhibited such determination to return to their ancestral home as the Cheyennes did.

Like other tribal people crushed by U.S. military power, the Cheyenne experience brought cries of mistreatment and massacre and demands that the circumstances be investigated. Even before the fighting stopped a three-man board met to examine the actions taken at Fort Robinson in response to charges from Washington about unusual cruelty toward the Northern Cheyenne prisoners. This board absolved the local officers of any wrongdoing and defended their actions as necessary under the circumstances. Newspapers across the country offered everything from racist anti-Indian attacks to sympathy for the Cheyennes and denunciations of the government. *Harper's Monthly Magazine* ran a series that examined national Indian policy critically, while the *New York Times* attacked the Office of Indian Affairs as being responsible for the tragedy. In 1879 the U.S. Senate established a Select Committee on the Removal of the Northern Cheyenne to investigate the incident.

Whether the attacks focused on the tribe, the army, or the Indian Office, the rhetoric failed to bring major changes. No one could argue that forcing the Cheyennes to leave their homeland and move south into Indian Territory resulted from anything but an uninformed policy implemented by unfeeling bureaucrats. The Indians in question spoke forcefully and repeatedly about wanting to leave the Indian Territory and return to land that they considered their home. The secretary of the interior, the commissioner of Indian Affairs, and their subordinates refused to listen to them, and the army had to police the western tribes without having much input into the process. Yet these people were not entirely innocent victims. Any honest look at their trek north has to recognize that along the way they committed murder, rape, arson, and robbery while spreading violence and terror among the mostly innocent frontier population. However, the troops at Fort Robinson had no reasons to justify their atrocities against their prisoners.

CHAPTER 10

Wounded Knee, 1890

It seems likely that more Americans have heard something about the massacre at Wounded Knee than about any other incident in American Indian history except for the Battle of the Little Bighorn, so it is fitting that this is the last one to be examined. The 1890 event at Wounded Knee Creek on the Pine Ridge Reservation in South Dakota brought two familiar groups—the Lakota Sioux and the U.S. Seventh Cavalry—together in the last major episode of the Indian wars. But it differed from many other fights because it happened as the army tried to avoid an Indian war, not begin one. It was also different because the fighting took place on the existing Pine Ridge Reservation against people whose only goal was religious, not military, and it occurred more than a decade after major fighting on the plains had ended. Unlike many of the other incidents, it took place in full view of newspaper reporters looking for a story. Whatever the circumstances, today most people accept the label "massacre" to describe the violence at Wounded Knee.

During the post–Civil War period, the Lakota Sioux represented the most serious obstacle to American expansion onto the northern plains. Ranging from Dakota west to Montana and south to Nebraska, they criss-crossed the region in pursuit of the vast buffalo herds and often warring with neighboring tribes. In theory they accepted the tribal borders negotiated in the 1868 Treaty of Fort Laramie. Yet the influx of white miners, homesteaders, and railroads into the region limited their movement and greatly reduced the buffalo herds.

In 1876, just over two months after the Indian victory at the Little Big-horn, George Manypenny led a commission to the new Red Cloud Agency in Dakota. The commissioners told their Indian listeners that Congress was taking a large part of the Great Sioux Reservation and that they had to surrender the Black Hills to the United States. When the chiefs objected, the whites threatened that Congress would cut off their food rations, send troops after them, and take the land no matter what the Indians did. Despite these threats the commissioners managed to get only about 10 percent of the men to sign the agreement, far short of the three-fourths of them required by the earlier Treaty of Fort Laramie. Despite the lack of Sioux consent. Congress broke that agreement and took the Black Hills and other parts of their land.[1]

Manypenny's negotiations opened the door. Soon other federal offi-cials visited the tribe, eager to get more land for the nearby rapidly grow-ing white settlements. Their efforts failed to meet settler demands. In 1882 Dakota's delegate to Congress called for a new effort to get Sioux lands. Soon the three newly appointed members of the Edmunds Com-mission made their way to Dakota and began visiting the Sioux agencies. They threatened the Sioux with deportation to the much-feared Indian Country, which had played such an important role in the Northern Cheyenne disaster at Fort Robinson. It is not entirely clear what the visi-tors told the Indians except that they needed them to agree to dividing Sioux lands into five separate reservations. Edmunds and his compan-ions failed to get three-quarters of the adult males to sign the agreement, but they hurried their results to Washington, D.C., anyway. A public out-cry and a Senate investigation undercut Edmunds's work and ended the new effort to take the tribe's land, but only temporarily.[2]

Continuing pressure from Dakota politicians and their supporters in Congress persuaded that body to establish another commission directed at getting the Sioux to cede more land. In 1889 President Benjamin Har-rison appointed the Crook Commission, led by General George Crook. Using the $250,000 Congress gave them, the commissioners hosted repeated feasts for the Indians and encouraged mixed-race people on the reservation to pressure their relatives to sign the new agreement. Still bound by the 1868 Fort Laramie Treaty requirement that they needed to get three-fourths of the men to sign any new agreement, the commissioners traveled from one agency to another, meeting Sioux leaders. They reminded the Indians that the government had the authority to end the treaty and take the land but said that they hoped the Sioux to would accept the terms being offered. These included creating five new smaller reservations where the Dawes Severalty Act would allot the land to each family. Congress had also raised the amount it would pay for the land taken and agreed to a $3 million permanent fund for the tribe. After months of haggling and persuasion in early August, Crook's efforts succeeded. The commissioners got 78 percent of the Sioux men to sign the new agreement. It erased the Great Sioux Reservation and created the five new smaller ones that exist today.[3]

The bitter debates in the late 1880s over whether to accept Crook's promises and sign the papers selling their lands made existing tensions between progressive and nonprogressive groups on the Sioux reservations worse. The parade of commissioners seeking land cessions during that decade disrupted village life already suffering from many stresses. Whites not only demanded tribal land but attacked Sioux culture from many directions. First, the Sioux had to surrender their horses and guns when the soldiers forced them onto the reservation. Having lived as part of a mounted, hunting-based culture, losing their mobility and the central way of feeding themselves disrupted much of their daily life. The Office of Indian Affairs attacked their religious practices and in 1883 outlawed the Sun Dance ceremonies. This further divided the villagers between those who accepted white people's Christianity and those who tried to follow their indigenous beliefs and ceremonies.[4] Arguments over white demands that the children attend school also divided the Indian communities.

Other events combined to turn the Indians' depression into desperation. Even without horses the men could still hunt, but nearly all of the big game had been killed. That left the Indians almost totally dependent on rations. However, the Sioux Act in 1889, which created Crook's commission to get tribal land, had also cut the amount of food that the government provided. That action, intended to coerce the Indians accept the land cession, increased misery on the reservation. Those people who had tried to farm faced a devastating drought that destroyed whatever crops they planted. Short of food from the government, and unable to either farm or hunt successfully, the Indians faced increasing malnutrition and sickness. As those circumstances became an everyday experience, the Sioux heard rumors of a new Indian messiah who promised a better life.[5]

By that time tales of an Indian messiah offering new teachings had circulated in the mountain West for several decades. In 1869–70 a Nevada Paiute named Wodziwob had preached about the return of all dead Indians and a mystical return to past cultural practices. In the late 1880s another Paiute named Wovoka offered similar teachings that attracted wide attention. He reported that a new messiah had come to earth and prophesized that soon the Indians would enjoy a life without death or sickness, the buffalo would return, and the Indians' relationship with nature would be renewed. In this new world the whites would disappear because of earthquakes, floods, or other natural disasters. To bring this about Indian believers were to dance and pray.[6]

When news of the new teachings reached the Sioux, some of them wanted to hear more about the new teacher and his ideas, so band leaders met. The councils at Pine Ridge, Rosebud, and Cheyenne River chose delegates to go west and investigate. The eleven men went to Wyoming, where they joined representatives from the Shoshoni, Northern Cheyenne, Arapaho, and Bannock tribes on their way to visit the new prophet. The group traveled by train and wagon to Walker Lake in western Nevada, where they met Wovoka. He told the visitors that during a January 1, 1889, eclipse of the sun he had a vision in which he died and went to heaven. There he met God, who gave him a message for the Indians. They had to remain at peace and to dance new rituals that the prophet would teach them. He called the ceremony the Ghost Dance, but the Sioux came to call it the Spirit Dance. They returned to their reservations, where Short Bull and Kicking Bear became the leaders in a new religious movement. They promised their followers that if they danced enough they could "die," have visions where they would see their dead friends and relatives, and visit the new life temporarily before returning to the present.[7]

Lakota responses to the delegates' reports varied widely. Some, like Short Bull and Kicking Bear, became major leaders of the dancing among the Lakotas. Others, such as Red Cloud, remained ambivalent about the new teachings. While he professed to be too old to dance in a discussion about it with General Nelson Miles, Red Cloud suggested that it resembled rites of the Roman Catholic Church. He told Miles that "their doctrines and belief and practice is [sic] what is taught by the scriptures." The canny leader hedged this apparent support by saying that "if it is true . . . it will go all over the world before it stops; on the other hand, if it is false . . . it will go away like the snow under the hot sun."[8] He clearly hoped to avoid a confrontation because of the dancers' activities.

Reception of the new teaching varied from one reservation to another, with many of the so-called nonprogressives—those who rejected acculturation—more likely to join the new dancing than their reservation opponents. Short Bull, both a Christian preacher and an accepted medicine man, led the dancers at Rosebud. Kicking Bear introduced the new ceremonies with such success at Cheyenne River that chiefs Big Foot and Hump presided over nearly continuous dancing. At Pine Ridge it took a few weeks longer to get the dances organized, but once begun they attracted most of the Indians there. The parish priest, Father Aemilius Perrig, complained that the dances had attracted all but six families of his church. He worried because "the appearing of Ghosts are [sic] said to express dislike for baptized persons, . . . the apparitions are inspiring the Indians with distrust, dislike, contempt or even hatred of the whites."[9]

The rapid spread of the dancing across the reservations upset the agents. They saw the ceremonies as just another backward indigenous rite that delayed the Indians' acceptance of Christianity and acculturation. Agent George Wright at Rosebud threatened dance leader Short Bull that he "would be a dead man" if he spread his ideas about the dance. In August 1890 Pine Ridge agent Hugh Gallagher sent some agency police to break up dances there. When they arrived, however, the over two thousand people who met them refused to stop, so the police left. Several weeks later agency officials visited another Ghost Dance site, this time to watch, not to stop it. Having failed to halt the dances or even reduce the number of Indians participating, agent Wright began to withhold food rations. But after a short time he lost his position, and the dances resumed. Whenever the agents moved to block the dances the Indians appeared fully armed and in such large numbers that the agency police feared to act against them.[10]

At Standing Rock tensions between agent James McLaughlin and Sitting Bull fed into the unrest and white panic over the Ghost Dance. Apparently the chief did not participate or even strongly support the dancers, but the agent worried about what he saw as the older Lakota chiefs' negative influence on the reservation. In a report to the acting commissioner of Indian Affairs, Robert Belt, he proposed "the removal from the reservation and confinement in some military prison . . . of Sitting Bull and the parties named in my [earlier] letter."[11] Belt suggested that the army arrest the chiefs, but military authorities declined to do so. As the whites argued over what to do and who should do it, more Indians joined the dances, defying Indian police efforts to end the ceremonies and ignoring threats of having their rations cut off.[12]

When more people took part in the dances and their leaders became more openly defiant, agency officials' complaints frightened people living in the nearby settlements. Responding to their demands on November 17, General Nelson Miles, commanding the Division of the Missouri, ordered General John Brooke to send troops to both the Pine Ridge and Rosebud reservations. Three days later 370 infantrymen and cavalry marched onto the Pine Ridge Agency grounds at dawn. That same morning 230 soldiers arrived at the Rosebud Agency grounds. Whatever thoughts the agents may have had about their ability to control the situation, federal authorities clearly felt less certain of their skills. The troops' appearance frightened many of the Sioux. Those who were not Ghost Dancers hurried their families to agency headquarters for protection. Determined to continue their religious ceremonies, the dancers ignored the troops and refused to end their dancing.[13]

Meanwhile, other soldiers moved to some of the nearby forts that ringed the Sioux reservations, At Standing Rock agent McLaughlin objected to having the army brought onto the reservation. Determined to seize control of the situation, he decided to arrest the older chiefs, believing that they blocked efforts to "civilize" the Sioux. To have the most impact, he chose the revered spiritual and political leader Sitting Bull as his first target. Working with Colonel William Drum at Fort Yates, he proposed using the agency police force to arrest the aging chief. When the colonel approved his plan, on December 14, 1890, the agent ordered agency police Lieutenant Henry Bull Head to use his men to arrest Sitting Bull.

Early the next morning the lieutenant led his 44-man detachment to Sitting Bull's house. There they found the chief and his family asleep. They ordered him to get dressed and step out of the cabin. While he dressed, his wife started to wail. The family dogs began barking, and the noise woke his neighbors. By the time the police got Sitting Bull out of the house, his guards had rallied and surrounded them. At that point the chief changed his mind and refused to cooperate. Even after Bull Head told him that he would not be hurt, the chief struggled and called for help. When Bull Head and several others grabbed Sitting Bull, his defenders began shooting at the police, who returned fire. In the melee that followed one of them shot Sitting Bull and seven of his defenders; seven of the policemen died in the melee. Not long after the firing ended, troops from Fort Yates arrived, adding to the Ghost Dancers' fears that the whites intended to kill them all.[14]

By allowing the Standing Rock police to arrest Sitting Bull and sending troops to the scene soon after his murder, Colonel Drum set the scene for the tragic and violent events that followed. During the next few weeks, new army units moved into Sioux country to strengthen the garrisons already there. Troop strength rose to more than 6,000 officers and men, clearly far more than the Sioux had. General Miles justified this massive buildup, reporting that he feared "the most serious Indian war of our history was imminent" and that many of the western settlements "were liable to be overrun by a hungry wild, mad horde of savages."[15] News of the fight at Standing Rock and the troop movements on the northern plains frightened some western settlers, but local town boosters worried more about the negative impact that Indian scares had on immigration into their communities than about any real danger from attacks.

Not surprisingly, the reservation dwellers feared the "Blue Coats," as they called the soldiers. Those most active in the Ghost Dance saw having army units on their reservations as a threat to their religious ceremonies. Some talked about fighting, others about fleeing to escape from the troops so that they could continue their dances. Before Sitting Bull's murder Red Cloud and other Oglala leaders offered Big Foot (Spotted Elk) 100 ponies to bring his Miniconjou band south to Pine Ridge. Big Foot had told Colonel Edwin Sumner that he would move east to Fort Bennett. But he decided to move south to Pine Ridge instead after Sitting Bull's death and reports from others that the troops there would take his followers' horses and guns. Sumner had orders to arrest the Miniconjou leader, but events and his attitude toward the Sioux kept him from doing that. While escorting the Indians toward his camp on December 22, Sumner's column led them past their village. Many of the women wanted to stop, and the chief asked him to let them remain. "This is their home, where the government has ordered them to stay, and none of my people have committed a single act requiring their removal by force," he told Sumner.[16] The colonel could only agree.

Sumner ordered Big Foot to come to his camp the next day and sent a local rancher John Dunn to tell the chief that the Miniconjous would have to follow the troops to Fort Bennett the next day. If they refused, the colonel threatened to force them to cooperate. By this time Big Foot had contracted pneumonia. While he missed the meeting with Sumner, he promised to travel east to the fort. Suspicious of the colonel's intentions, the other Miniconjou leaders debated what to do. Some wanted to stay in their village, while others suggested traveling to either the fort or to Pine Ridge. Unable to agree, they moved into the hills. When troops came looking for them, they decided to accept Red Cloud's invitation. They sent word that "Big Foot was on his way to the Agency, and was very sick" and expected to arrive "openly and peacefully."[17]

Instead of meeting the colonel as promised and fearing that the troops would attack, the Miniconjous slipped away late in the evening of December 23, leaving the soldiers empty handed. Having heard that Colonel Sumner had captured Big Foot's band, only to learn that they had escaped, General Miles replaced Sumner and ordered a major search for the fugitives. For several days the Indians managed to avoid their pursuers while moving toward Pine Ridge. Then on December 28 four army scouts saw the Indian camp. Big Foot told them that the Miniconjous expected to come directly to his camp. Late that afternoon the soldiers and Indians met. Both lined up for battle, but Big Foot had a white flag flying over his wagon, which was driven up to the troops. Major Samuel Whiteside, the commanding officer, told the ailing chief that he had to take his people to Wounded Knee Creek and that the soldiers would take the Indians' horses and weapons. His scout John Shangreau protested: "Look here, Major, if you do that there is liable to be a fight here; and if there is you will kill all those women and children and the men will get away."[18]

The major agreed and told Big Foot to take his people and camp along the creek. Seeing how sick the chief was, Whiteside had him moved to an army medical wagon for a more comfortable ride during the five-mile trip to Wounded Knee Creek. When they halted for the night, the colonel posted guards around Big Foot's tent. He reported having taken the Miniconjous prisoners. He asked for rations to feed them and had tents pitched for them, but the Sioux used their own tepees. When White-side called for reinforcements, Colonel James Forsyth's troops from the Seventh Cavalry came to guard the camp with its 120 men and 230 women and children. The soldiers arrived by evening and quietly surrounded the Indians. Big Foot's followers spent a nearly sleepless night wondering whether the soldiers would kill them in the morning, while Forsyth completed his plans to disarm them.[19]

Forsythe's command of nearly 500 men consisted mostly of cavalry, with a small detachment of artillery and 30 scouts. Weaker than it might seem, his force included about 80 untrained recruits and 30 Oglala scouts, who were not likely to willingly shoot their friends and relatives. The soldiers each had a single-shot rifle and a six-shot revolver. That made them less well armed than the Sioux, who had repeating Winchester rifles. However, the troops had several artillery pieces, which more than anything gave them superior firepower. Forsyth deployed his mounted units to surround the Indian camp. Then he placed the artillery on a nearby hill. General John Brooke, the local commander, had warned the colonel "to take every precaution to prevent escape of any of Big Foot's people, and to be particularly careful in disarming them."[20] This directive echoed General Miles's earlier order to capture and disarm Big Foot's people. "If he fights, destroy him," the general had instructed.[21]

The next morning, December 29, the troops woke to "Reveille" at 5:15 as Colonel Forsyth began his plan to disarm the prisoners. Some of the soldiers gave the Indians breakfast, while others prepared to gather their weapons. Soon after the meal two observers from several nearby towns and three newspaper reporters rode up to the camp to watch. When the colonel called for the Miniconjou men to assemble in front of Big Foot's tent, 106 of them stood, sat, or squatted there on the ground. Forsyth told them that they were prisoners and had to surrender their guns but that they would be well treated once they moved to Pine Ridge. He assured them that "they were perfectly safe in the hands of their old friends the soldiers, and that starvation and other troubles were now happily at an end."[22] As soon as they gave up the last of their guns, he would lead them to the agency.

Forsyth's demand that they surrender their weapons struck directly at part of what was left of Sioux cultural identity. They had surrendered much of their land, their independence, and most of their ponies: now the whites demanded their prized and expensive weapons. Believing that the whites had lied to them repeatedly, they put little faith in promises that their captors would treat them kindly once they had been disarmed.[23] Many of the young men considered their rifles to be a part of their identity as hunters and fighting men. The rifle was also the most expensive thing they owned, and many objected to surrendering the guns even though the colonel had promised to compensate them later. When Forsyth demanded all the guns in the Indian camp, Big Foot warned his followers to cooperate. "My sons," he said, "I am thinking some trouble will come to us. Whatever the soldiers tell you to do, I want you to do it, and do not do anything that will give the soldiers an excuse to hurt you."[24]

At that point the colonel sent twenty of the Miniconjou men back to their tents to gather their guns. They returned with two old broken carbines. When Forsyth objected, Big Foot claimed that the men in his camp had surrendered all the weapons a few days earlier, so now they had none to turn over. Colonel Forsyth instructed the translator to "tell Big Foot that he tells me that his Indians have no arms when yesterday at the time of surrender they were well armed. I am sure he is deceiving me."[25] The Sioux remembered the situation differently. Rather than surrendering only a few useless guns, they claimed that the young men had gone back to the camp and returned with twenty-five rifles. When the officer took the weapons, he asked the Indians to bring five more, which they did. Then they reported that "there are no more guns" in the camp. Although they had cooperated up to that point, some of the Indians had no intention of surrendering their weapons. For example, Dewey Beard dug a hole in the tent floor and covered his with dirt. Then he hid the cartridges in a small pile of manure. He was not the only one who did this, because when the fighting began the Miniconjous still had enough weapons to kill many of the soldiers.[26]

When Forsyth and his officer decided that the Indians had hidden some of their weapons, they sent men to search the individual tents. The searchers went through the Indians' bundles of clothing, food, and blankets, often pulling them out from under the objecting women. One of the men reported that the "squaws [made] every effort to conceal [weapons], by hiding them and sitting on them." He found a gun "under the skirts of a squaw, and we had to throw her on her back to get it."[27] With the troops nervous about Indian behavior and Big Foot's followers angry and frightened by the soldiers' actions, tensions mounted. One of the Ghost Dance leaders chanted, threw dirt into the air, and shouted not to give their last weapons to the soldiers. When several soldiers walked up to some of the Indian men, demanding they remove their blankets to prove they had no weapons hidden under them, one Indian recounted that Black Fox waved them off, saying, "Keep away from me. I will die before I will let you have my gun, and if I die I will take some of you with me."[28]

At that point the soldiers tried to wrestle the rifle out of his hands, and it went off. Father Francis Craft, who had been brought to the camp to help calm the tensions, remembered the start of the fighting differently. Instead of Black Fox's rifle being fired by accident, he said that the young man fired the first shot at the soldiers and that immediately five or six other Sioux men threw off their blankets and began firing too. That set off a murderous volley from the troops toward any of the Indians standing there and into the tents too. The Miniconjou men grabbed whatever weapons they could, often taking the dead soldiers' weapons and cartridge belts as they tried to defend their camp. When the shooting began, Indians scattered quickly, some fleeing into a nearby ravine or any other place that offered shelter. According to Captain Charles Varnum, the fighting began with "one deafening crash" that knocked down nearly thirty Indians and cut through the ranks of soldiers too. One of the newspapermen reported: "In a moment the whole front was a sheet of fire above which the smoke rolled, obscuring the central scene." Then "the Indians fired outward in all directions as along the spokes from the hub of a wheel. Soldiers also fired inwardly."[29]

This set off a wild melee, with soldiers shooting at anything or anyone that moved, Indians targeting anything in blue, and women screaming and children crying as they tried to flee. A Sioux participant later recalled that he "saw solders on both sides of the ravine shoot at them until they had killed every one of them."[30] from the wounded and dead people spread all over the ground. Within a few minutes the soldiers' heavy rifle fire and the destructive blasts of the Hotchkiss guns tore the tents to shreds. Colonel Forsyth's poor placement of his troops may have caused the soldiers to kill and wound some of their own men. The soldiers chased the fleeing Indians. Sporadic firing continued until early afternoon. By then Forsyth's force had lost twenty-nine men and one Indian scout. The number of Miniconjou fatalities remains uncertain. Many of the wounded escaped but died later. At the scene the victors counted the bodies of eighty-five men and sixty-eight women and children. Some of the Indian dead had tried to escape and perished in the brush or other hiding places that they found. The final death count included another forty-seven Miniconjous listed without age or sex.[31] By the end of the day Big Foot's band no longer existed.

Taking care of the wounded became a major task at the agency. The wounded soldiers lay in large floored tents designed to house up to sixty patients; warmed by large stoves, they got the latest treatments. At the battlefield the troops gathered the bodies of their comrades and took them back to the agency. Later they moved the corpses to the Pine Ridge cemetery for a military burial ceremony. The Lakotas got much less reverential treatment. The army placed the wounded Indians in a quickly organized temporary hospital in the local Episcopal church. A week later the church staff moved the injured to the nearby mission school. A burial detail placed the dead Indians in a long trench that served as their grave, located on what became known as cemetery hill on the reservation.

On January 1, 1891, Sioux agency physician Charles Eastman (himself a Sioux), some of the Indian scouts, and a few other Indians took wagons out to the battle scene, looking for Indian survivors. They found some hidden in an abandoned shack and others scattered in the brush and rescued eleven people, including two infants, from almost certain death. Eastman described the snow-covered battle site as "a terrible and horrible sight, to see women and children lying in groups, dead. . . . In front of the tents, which were in a semi-circle, lay dead most of the men." A reporter for the *Omaha World-Herald* who accompanied the burial detail described seeing "children of an age to play tag in a city . . . boys, down to the ages of 10 and 11, who wore gaudy painted ghost shirts . . . lay everywhere, half buried under the snow."[32]

There is no credible evidence that the army planned to kill or do anything more than disarm the Big Foot's followers at Wounded Knee. In attempting to do that, they followed the standard practice that the troops had used since 1876–77 when Indians surrendered. They collected their horses and weapons as a part of the effort to cut their mobility and force them to become farmers or stock raisers. In this case a few of the young men, perhaps afraid that the soldiers would kill them, may have decided that they would shoot a few of the whites before dying or returned fire when the soldiers' attack began. The conflicting evidence about who fired first makes it impossible to place blame for starting the fighting with any certainty. However, it seems clear that the agency officials' panicky over-reaction to the dances led directly to the disaster.

Both national and local newspapers reported the event thoroughly, but their coverage failed to provoke any mass public outrage or defense of the troops. They denounced the government's ineffective policies and criticized it for failing to live up to promises to feed Indians when they settled on reservations. A few censured the army for having so many sol-diers at the scene, suggesting that their presence had led to the violence. When news of the disaster hit, American officials tried to deflect blame for the tragedy. President Benjamin Harrison complained that General Miles had failed to avoid bloodshed. Miles shifted the blame by attacking Colonel Forsyth, relieving him of his command, and calling for an inves-tigation. Except for the Apaches trying to flee their Arizona reservations, major Indian wars had ended in the last 1870s. News of Wounded Knee failed to raise the level of protests or even public interest evoked by some of the earlier massacres.[33]

Long-time government critic Herbert Welsh of the Indian Rights Association denounced the Ghost Dance leaders and called for them to be punished. At the same time, he asked Captain John Bourke, former aid to General George Crook and a man with long experience in Indian matters, to investigate. As part of his inquiry in February 1891 the cap-tain met with Métis Baptiste Pourier and Louis Richard and Louis Shan-greau, both Lakota mixed-bloods who had been at the scene. They repeated Elaine Goodale's earlier charges that the soldiers had deliber-ately killed Sioux women and children. Shangreau and his companions accused the soldiers of having "murdered [the Indians] wherever they caught up with them, in ravines, gulches, or other places to which they were retreating for safety."[34] Soon after their meeting *Washington Evening Star* reporter George Harries reinforced Bourke's accounts. Harries had been at Pine Ridge and described *how "there were women and children killed in cold blood;*—children of three years shot as a test of marksmanship." He defended that statement, saying that he had "heard the story from the soldier's own lips."[35] Whether this was fact or just post-battle bragging, Bourke clearly believed the testimony.

Except for some minor skirmishing in the few days after Wounded Knee, the fighting there ended the Indian Wars. In the late nineteenth century Wounded Knee received less national attention than had a number of the earlier massacres. Perhaps this was because it had not resulted from any campaign to defeat and capture marauding bands of mounted Indians seen as endangering pioneer settlers or miners. Most Americans who knew anything about the incident considered it the result of an obscure Indian religious movement, not a matter of public safety. The conflict pitted the soldiers against a group of people who had already surrendered and were traveling to a reservation, not fleeing from one. The bloodshed, when it came, resulted from careless planning, confusion, and just plain bad luck, not from any planned attack or Indian belligerence. What comes down to us as the Wound Knee Massacre shows how unexpected actions turned what was supposed to be a peaceful surrender into a battle that then shifted into a massacre in the heat of combat.

Conclusion

Looking at American history from the twenty-first century, it is easy to criticize past government ideas and actions. We are used to viewing the programs and actions of a massive bureaucracy, making it difficult to accept that in the nineteenth century it was far smaller, weaker, and even less competent than the blundering giant we see today. In the age of computers we experience instant communication and rapid movement of goods and people around the country. However, the world 150 years ago was a vastly different place. Technologically backward and poorly governed, it was frequently overwhelmed by the challenges of dealing with the Indians. Before the 1870s stagecoaches and freight wagons carried the mail. Steamboats carried people and goods on the rivers, but often only in the spring and summer. In winter many rivers froze, in spring they flooded, and in late summer they lacked enough water to make navigation possible. Even after railroads crossed much of the West and telegraph wires connected most of the country, the size of the continent hindered the effective movement of people and information. In these circumstances and with the society and its leaders divided sharply over how to deal with the Indians, federal policies and actions failed and helped to cause the massacres discussed here.

Public responses to them support my contention that American society conducted Indian affairs and responded to news of victories over tribal peoples in a schizophrenic haze. Few people either in or out of government had an informed understanding of the issues resulting from the settler colonialism that marked national policies. In their determination to control the national domain, federal policy makers developed programs to encourage white settlement in Indian homelands without careful thought about the results. Like any people being invaded, the indigenous groups objected to the presence and actions of the pioneers. They rejected demands to surrender their best hunting lands and criticized invading whites on the overland trails for killing their game, taking the firewood, destroying the grass their horses needed, and inflicting unpredictable violence on Indians who met them.

The nineteenth-century interracial violence created situations where attacking forces of both whites and Indians committed atrocities and massacres. In the ten incidents examined here the U.S. military forces varied:

In the Red Stick War: regular troops, state militia, and Indian allies
In the Black Hawk War: regular troops, state militia, and Indian allies
At Ash Hollow: regular troops
At Bear River: California Volunteers
At Sand Creek: Colorado Volunteers
At the Washita: regular troops and Osage scouts
At the Marias River: regular troops
At Skeleton Cave: regular troops and Apache scouts
At Fort Robinson: regular troops
At Wounded Knee: regular troops

This list suggests that regular troops, at times assisted by Indian scouts, committed all but two of the massacres. The volunteers perpetrated the massacres at Bear River and Sand Creek. The postbattle atrocities connect the militiamen in the Red Stick and Black Hawk Wars with the volunteers already mentioned. Usually the U.S. Regulars had orders to avoid killing women and children, but in one instance a unit specifically hunted and killed them. In other attacks some of the troops fired into the lodges where the women and children hid and shot many of them. At the same time, most of them avoided committing atrocities in their victories. In fact, they rescued abandoned children and gave people with minor wounds medical attention. Clearly, officers leading the militiamen and volunteers exercised less control over the violent behavior of their men. Indian allies and scouts both followed their own military practices, which included scalping and rendering enemy corpses unfit for the afterlife. Both of those practices would have been atrocities if committed by whites. When the fights ended, these groups all had inflicted horrendous destruction on the indigenous camps that they destroyed.

These massacres happened in highly charged situations. Throughout the nineteenth century both the Indians and the invading whites had intense negative ethnocentric and racist ideas of each other. Settlers living near or having to deal with the indigenous people considered them to be dirty, lazy, drunken, nearly naked, dangerous "savages," people who could not be trusted or civilized and certainly not desirable future neighbors. Indians' experiences with pioneers and frontier area officials produced equally damning views of their white neighbors. They considered federal negotiators to be liars and thieves who promised much but delivered little. The American actions that encouraged them to accept schools, churches, and farming equipment, while at the same time demanding that they either surrender their land or move, seemed schizophrenic. They saw the pioneers as dangerous, selfish, greedy, dishonest, and a threat to their food supplies.

In each of the cases examined here, violent actions by both sides led to calls for punishing or destroying the Indians. That resulted in situations where military authorities failed to differentiate between those guilty of raiding and others who just happened to be in the way of armed forces sent to retaliate. Tribal customs demanding blood revenge for outsiders' attacks or injury to friends or relatives produced a cycle of attack and retaliation that enemy tribes recognized. U.S. authorities tried to end this custom: clauses in many of the treaties that chiefs signed demanded that village leaders prohibit their people from carrying out their clan obligations. American negotiators who made those demands rejected the idea that the chiefs had no power to stop village members from responding to such incidents. So chiefs who claimed to be working for peace often appeared to be liars who secretly harbored young men guilty of raiding.

When troops attacked villages or camps of people who thought they were at peace or assaulted the wrong village, they caught the Indians almost totally unprepared and nearly defenseless. In those cases the Indians had not taken their usual steps to protect the women and children from danger, leading to high casualties of noncombatants. The army's resort to winter raids on Indian camps produced similarly high numbers of victims. The challenging winter weather limited the villagers' mobility and made them much easier to find than during the summer. In winter the Indians had fewer men out as hunters or scouts, who might have seen the troops and been able to warn the villagers in time for them to escape and avoid the attack. These events provide clear examples of military attacks on Indian communities that descended into brutal massacres, events that no American can look at with pride.

Notes

INTRODUCTION

1. *Merriam-Webster*, s.v. "massacre," accessed December 10 2018, https://www.merriam-webster.com/dictionary/massacre; Wilhelm, *A Military Dictionary*, 310.

2. Quoted in Madley, *An American Genocide*, 46–48.

3. Wolfe, "Settler Colonialism."

4. Hatch, *Black Kettle*; Nichols, *Lincoln and the Indians*; Prucha, *Great Father*; Berkhofer, *White Man's Indian*.

5. Anderson, *Ethnic Cleansing*.

6. Jefferson to Henry Dearborn, August 28, 1807, Jefferson, *Writings*, 11:344.

7. Power, *"Problem from Hell"*; Stannard, *American Holocaust*; Thornton, *American Indian Holocaust*.

8. Ostler, "Genocide and American Indian History," 9.

9. Clifton, *Being and Becoming Indian*, 6.

10. "Declaration of Independence," in *Federal and State Constitutions*, ed. Thorpe, 5.

11. Black Hawk, *Black Hawk: An Autobiography* (hereafter *Autobiography*); Nichols, *American Indians in U.S. History*.

12. Ostler, "Genocide and American Indian History," 9.

13. Washington to James Duane, September 7, 1783, Fitzpatrick, *Writings of George Washington*, 27:140.

14. Washington to Timothy Pickering, July 1, 1796, Fitzpatrick, *Writings of George Washington*, 35:112.

15. U.S. Bureau of the Census, *Report on Indians*, 637.

16. Coffman, *Old Army*; Hutton, *Phil Sheridan*; Osborn, *The Wild Frontier*; Matt Remle, "Mass Killings, Native Erasure," https://lastrealindians.com/news/2016/6 /21/jun-21-2016-mass-killings-native-erasure-by-matt-remle, accessed June 16, 2020; "List of Indian Massacres," https://en.wikipedia.org/wiki/List_of_Indian _massacres, accessed June 16, 2020.

17. Commager, *Documents of American History*, p. 141.

18. Quoted in Reston, *Sherman's March*, 40.

19. Weigley, *American Way of War*, 82–87.

20. Janda, "Shutting the Gates," 10 (quotation), 13–15.

21. Sheridan, *Personal Memoirs*, 1:488.

CHAPTER 1. RED STICK WAR

1. Crockett, *Life*, 88–90.

2. Doherty, *Richard Keith Call*, 6.

3. Waselkov, *Conquering Spirit*, 163; Owsley, *The Struggle for the Gulf Borderlands*, 65.

4. Waselkov, *Conquering Spirit*, 99.

5. Halbert and Ball, *Creek War*, 147–48; Waselkov, *Conquering Spirit*, 114–15.

6. Ethridge, *Creek Country*, 26–27; Waselkov, *Conquering Spirit*, 89–100, 116–20; Saunt, *New Order*, 259–63, 267–70.

7. Owsley, *Struggle for the Gulf Borderlands*, 43.

8. Ethridge, *Creek Country*, 25–31; Frank, *Creeks and Southerners*, 11–25; Green, *Politics of Indian Removal*, 4–24.

9. Frank, *Creeks and Southerners*, 11–25; Green, *Politics of Indian Removal*, 4–25.

10. Saunt, *New Order*, 69–75. See also Caughey, *McGillivray*, 1–57.

11. Quoted in Green, "Alexander McGillivray," 48.

12. Green, "Alexander McGillivray," 48.

13. Quoted in Wright, *Creeks and Seminoles*, 136.

14. Kappler, *Indian Affairs*, 2:25–29.

15. Martin, *Sacred Revolt*, 95; Dowd, *Spirited Resistance*, 148–57.

16. Waselkov provides a careful analysis in *Conquering Spirit*, chapter 2.

17. Martin, *Sacred Revolt*, 120–21.

18. Benjamin Hawkins to William Eustis, September 21, 1811, in Hawkins, *Letters, Journals, and Writings*, 2:591–92; Martin, *Sacred Revolt*, 121–22.

19. Quoted in Martin, *Sacred Revolt*, 120.

20. Sugden, *Tecumseh*, 237–49.

21. Sugden, *Tecumseh*, 242, 244.

22. Sugden, *Tecumseh*, 146–47, 230–31, 249–51.

23. Martin *Sacred Revolt*, 123–24; Waselkov, *Conquering Spirit*, 88.

24. Saunt, *New Order*, 251–52.

25. Quoted in Florette Henri, *The Southern Indians and Benjamin Hawkins*, 265.

26. Waselkov, *Conquering Spirit*, 89, 91–95; Martin, *Sacred Revolt*, 127–28; Saunt, *New Order*, 253–59.

27. Owsley, *Struggle for the Gulf Borderlands*, 18–29.

28. Quoted in Kanon, "Slow, Laborious Slaughter," 13, note 4.

29. Crockett, *Life*, 92–93.

30. Griffith, *McIntosh and Weatherford*, 120–122.

31. Quoted in Halbert and Ball, *Creek War*, 272; Griffith, *McIntosh and Weatherford*, 123.

32. Borneman, *1812: The War That Forged a Nation*, 150.

33. Kanon, "Slow, Laborious Slaughter," 9.

34. Kanon, "Slow, Laborious Slaughter," 9, 10.

35. Kanon, "Slow, Laborious Slaughter," 10.

36. Halbert and Ball, *Creek War*, 276; Takaki, *Different Mirror*, 85.

CHAPTER 2. BAD AXE

1. Black Hawk, *Autobiography*, 51.

2. Jung, *Black Hawk War*, 169–72; Hall, *Uncommon Defense*, 195–98.

3. Quoted in Jung, *Black Hawk War*, 173.

4. Black Hawk, *Autobiography*, 51.

5. Amos Stoddard to William Claiborne, March 26, 1804, quoted in *Glimpses of the Past* 2, no. 2 (May–September 1935): 98.

6. The situation has been well explained in Hagan, *Sac and Fox Indians*; Hall, *Uncommon Defense*; Jung, *Black Hawk War*; Nichols, *General Henry Atkinson*.

7. Wallace, "Prelude to Disaster," 1:17.

8. Warren Cattle to James Bruff, September 9, 1804, in Carter and Bloom, *Territorial Papers*, 13:62.

9. James Bruff to James Wilkinson, November 5, 1804, in Carter and Bloom, *Territorial Papers*, 13:76–80.

10. James Bruff to James Wilkinson, November 5, 1804, in Carter and Bloom, *Territorial Papers*, 13:57–58; Black Hawk, *Autobiography*, 53; Cole, *I Am a Man*, 30–31.

11. Wallace, "Prelude to Disaster," 1:18–21.

12. Kappler, "Sacs and Foxes Treaty, November 3, 1804," in *Indian Affairs*, 2:54–56.

13. Black Hawk, *Autobiography*, 55–58.

14. Quoted in Hagan, *Sac and Fox Indians*, 44.

15. Wallace, "Prelude to Disaster," 1:17–18.

16. Black Hawk, *Autobiography*, 62–63.

17. Black Hawk, *Autobiography*, 63–66.

18. Black Hawk, *Autobiography*, 60.

19. Black Hawk, *Autobiography*, 72–73; Hagan, *Sac and Fox Indians*, 88–89.

20. Black Hawk, *Autobiography*, 78–81; Jung, *Black Hawk War*, 29; Hagan, *Sac and Fox Indians*, 64–72.

21. Prucha, *Guide*, 57, 68, 79, 108.

22. Black Hawk, *Autobiography*, 88.

23. Hagan, *Sac and Fox Indians*, 90.

24. Quoted in Hagan, *Sac and Fox Indians*, 90.

25. Hagan, *Sac and Fox Indians*, 90; Nichols, *Black Hawk*, 69–72; and Hagan, *Sac and Fox Indians*, 95.

26. Kappler, "Sacs and Foxes Treaty," Article 5, p. 55.

27. Hagan, *Sac and Fox Indians*, 95.

28. *American State Papers*, 2:588–90; Foley, *Wilderness Journey*, 239.

29. Wallace, "Prelude to Disaster," 1:25; Nichols, *Black Hawk*, 75–78.

30. Black Hawk, *Autobiography*, 101.

31. Wallace, "Prelude to Disaster," 1:30.

32. Black Hawk, *Autobiography*, 105–6.

33. Black Hawk, *Autobiography*, 101, 113.

34. Taimah and Appenose to William Clark, July 22, 1832, in Whitney, *Black Hawk War*, 2:852–53.

35. Wallace, "Prelude to Disaster," 1:32–33.

36. Black Hawk, *Autobiography*, 101.

37. Quoted in Wallace, "Prelude to Disaster," 1:42.

38. Hagan, *Sac and Fox Indians*, 143–59; Hall, *Uncommon Defense*, 121–34.

39. Black Hawk, *Autobiography*, 120–22.

40. Jung, *Black Hawk War*, 78–79; Trask, *Black Hawk*, 183, 186; Hall, *Uncommon Defense*, 133–34.

41. Jung, *Black Hawk War*, 114–15.

42. Jung, *Black Hawk War*, 153–56; Trask, *Black Hawk*, 260–61.

43. Nichols, *Black Hawk*, 141; Trask, *Black Hawk*, 266.

44. Hall, *Uncommon Defense*, 193–94.

45. Jung, *Black Hawk War*, 164–66, 170–71; Trask, *Black Hawk*, 279.

46. Jung, *Black Hawk War*, 169–72; Hall, *Uncommon Defense*, 195–98.

CHAPTER 3. ASH HOLLOW

1. Quoted in Adams, *General William S. Harney*, 129.

2. Quoted in Utley, *Frontiersmen in Blue*, 115.

3. Quoted in Clow, "Mad Bear," 140; see also Adams, *General William S. Harney*, 151.

4. Beck, *First Sioux War*, 102.

5. Quoted in Mattison, "Harney Expedition," 114.

6. Quoted in Paul, *Blue Water Creek*, 101.

7. Quoted in Beck, *First Sioux War*, 103.

8. Quoted in Ostler, *Plains Sioux*, 41. For detaied accounts of the attack see Paul, *Blue Water Creek*, 88–110, and Greene, *January Moon*, 27–48.

9. Quoted in Adams, *General William S. Harney*, 132–33.

10. Kvasnicka and Viola, *Commissioners of Indian Affairs*, 43; Prucha, *Guide to the Military Posts*, 82, 84.

11. Quoted in Fowler et al., *Arapahoe Politics*, 56.

12. Kappler, *Indian Affairs*, 2:594–95.

13. Prucha, *American Indian Treaties*, 238–40.

14. *Cherokee v. Georgia*, 30 U.S. (5 Pet.) 1 (1831).

15. Price examines this issue in "Lakota and Euro-Americans."

16. Ewers, "Intertribal Warfare."

17. Beck, *First Sioux War*, 39–41.

18. Beck, *First Sioux War*, 41–42; Paul, *Blue Water Creek*, 18; Utley, *Frontiersmen in Blue*, 114.

19. Quoted in Beck, *First Sioux War*, 46.

20. Quoted in Beck, *First Sioux War*, 48.

21. Quoted in Beck, *First Sioux War*, 51.

22. Paul, *Blue Water Creek*, 22–25; Beck, *First Sioux War*, 55–61; Utley, *Frontiersmen in Blue*, 114; McCann, "Grattan Massacre."

23. Beck, *First Sioux War*, 65–66.

24. Quoted in Beck, *First Sioux War*, 65.

25. Beck, *First Sioux War*, 67–69 (quotations); Adams, *General William S. Harney*, 121; Paul, *Blue Water Creek*, 32.

26. Beck, *First Sioux War*, 69–71.

27. Quoted in Paul, *Blue Water Creek*, 33.

28. Quoted in Adams, *General William S. Harney*, 124–25.

29. Quoted in Clow, "Mad Bear," 134.

30. Beck, *First Sioux War*, 78–83; Paul, *Blue Water Creek*, 36–37; Clow, "Mad Bear," 134–36.

31. Quoted in Paul, *Blue Water Creek*, 93.

32. Clow, "Mad Bear," 138; Paul, *Blue Water Creek*, 92–94.

33. Quoted in Adams, *General William S. Harney*, 127. See also Utley, *Frontiersmen in Blue*, 115–16; Paul, *Blue Water Creek*, 57–62.

34. Clow, "Mad Bear," 145–47.

CHAPTER 4. BEAR RIVER

1. Utley, *Frontiersmen in Blue*, 216–17.

2. Utley, *Frontiersmen in Blue*, 216.

3. Madsen, *Glory Hunter*, 13–18, 20–24, 49–57.

4. Quoted in Fleisher, *Bear River Massacre*, 49.

5. Quoted in Madsen, *Glory Hunter*, 85–86.

6. Christensen, *Sagwitch*, 4–5.

7. Unruh, *Plains Across*, 185.

8. Madsen, *Shoshoni Frontier*, 17; Christensen, *Sagwitch*, 3–4.

9. Quoted in Christensen, *Sagwitch*, 16.

10. Christensen, *Sagwitch*, 19, 22.

11. Unruh, *Plains Across*, 187.

12. Quoted in Unruh, *Plains Across*, 187.

13. Shannon, *Boise Massacre*, 74–75.

14. Shannon, *Boise Massacre*, 75, 78–79.

15. Shannon, *Boise Massacre*, 95–97.

16. Shannon, *Utter Disaster*, 33–45.

17. Shannon, *Utter Disaster*, 44–74, 74.

18. Quoted in Utley, *Frontiersmen in Blue, 223.*

19. Madsen, *Shoshoni Frontier*, 168.

20. Quoted in Madsen, *Shoshoni Frontier*, 178–79.

21. Madsen, *Shoshoni Frontier*, 182–83.

22. Quoted in Madsen, *Shoshoni Frontier,* 189. Madsen gives the most accurate discussion of the attack.

23. Quoted in Madsen, *Shoshoni Frontier*, 191, 193.

24. Quoted in Madsen, *Shoshoni Frontier*, 194.

25. Madsen, *Shoshoni Frontier*, 196.

26. Fleisher, *Bear River Massacre*, 66.

CHAPTER 5. SAND CREEK

1. Hoig, *Sand Creek Massacre*, 194; Hatch, *Black Kettle*, 167–84. The most recent treatment of this event is Kraft, *Sand Creek.*

2. "Treaty of Fort Laramie, 1851," in Kappler, *Indian Affairs*, 2:77–81.

3. Grinnell, *Fighting Cheyennes*, 111–12; Hyde, *Life of George Bent*, 100; Powell, *People of the Sacred Mountain*, 1:202–203.

4. Berthrong, *Southern Cheyennes,* 133–36; West, *Contested Plains*, 1–2; Grinnell, *Fighting Cheyennes*, 112–13; Commissioner of Indian Affairs, *Annual Report* (1856).

5. Berthrong, *Southern Cheyennes*, 133–36.

6. Chalfant's *Cheyennes and Horse Soldiers* is the most thorough account of Sumner's moves.

7. Quoted in Hatch, *Black Kettle*, 73–74.

8. "Treaty of Fort Wise," in Kappler, *Indian Affairs*, 2:807–11; Berthrong, *Southern Cheyennes*, 149–50; West, *Contested Plains*, 281–83.

9. "Treaty of Fort Wise," in Kappler, *Indian Affairs*, 2:807–11.

10. Quoted in Hoig, *Peace Chiefs*, 72. See also Viola, *Diplomats in Buckskin*, 99–102.

11. Quoted in Berthrong, *Southern Cheyennes*, 168. See also Commissioner of Indian Affairs, *Annual Report* (1863), 129–130.

12. Berthrong, *Southern Cheyennes*, 172; West, *Contested Plains*, 284–85; Commissioner of Indian Affairs, *Annual Report* (1863), 224–25.

13. Quoted in Grinnell, *Fighting Cheyennes*, 134–35. See also Berthrong, *Southern Cheyennes*, 172.

14. Quoted in Svaldi, *Sand Creek*, 150.

15. Berthrong, *Southern Cheyennes*, 173; Hatch, *Back Kettle*, 106.

16. Commissioner of Indian Affairs, *Annual Report* (1863), 393.

17. Hatch, *Black Kettle*, 109–10, 112–13.

18. Quoted in Hatch, *Black Kettle*, 117.

19. Hatch, *Black Kettle*, 117–20.

20. Kraft, *Sand Creek*, 138–39.

21. Quoted in Kraft, *Sand Creek*, 123–24. See also West, *Contested Plains*, 290–95.

22. Kraft, *Sand Creek*, 126–27.

23. Hoig quotes the council discussion in *Sand Creek Massacre*, 116–160. Chivington's comment is quoted in Hoig, *Sand Creek Massacre*, 20.

24. Hatch, *Black Kettle*, 141–42.

25. Hatch, *Black Kettle*, notes 27, 28, 29 on p. 281.

26. Quoted in Lecompte, "Sand Creek," 334.

CHAPTER 6. WASHITA RIVER

1. Quoted in Hutton, *Phil Sheridan*, 63.

2. Hatch, *Black Kettle*, 249–51.

3. Hardorff, *Washita Memories*, 393–98.

4. Donovan, *Terrible Glory*, 253; Robinson, *Good Year to Die*, 257.

5. Quoted in Greene, *Washita*, 24.

6. "Little Arkansas Treaty," in Kappler, *Indian Affairs*, 2:876–82.

7. Quoted in Berthrong, *Southern Cheyennes*, 242.

8. Greene, *Washita*, 29–31.

9. Quoted in Berthrong, *Southern Cheyennes*, 268.

10. Greene, *Washita*, 31–33; Hatch, *Black Kettle*, 213–25.

11. Monnett, in *Battle of Beecher Island*, gives a full account of this incident. See also Hoig, *Battle of the Washita*, 55–66.

12. Hatch, *Black Kettle*, 27–32.

13. Quoted in Hoig, *Battle of the Washita*, 35.

14. Greene, *Washita*, 37–238; Hatch, *Black Kettle*, 227–32.

15. Hoig, *Battle of the Washita*, 46–47.

16. Quoted in Greene, *Washita*, 48.

17. Quoted in Greene, *Washita*, 49.

18. Greene, *Washita*, 61.

19. Quoted in Greene, *Washita*, 50.

20. Quoted in Hoig, *Battle of the Washita*, 53.

21. Quoted in Hoig, *Battle of the Washita*, 69.

22. Quoted in Hatch, *Black Kettle*, 240.

23. Quoted in Hutton, *Phil Sheridan*, 57–59.

24. Hatch, *Black Kettle*, 237.

25. Quoted in Hutton, *Phil Sheridan*, 59.

26. Hoig, *Battle of the Washita*, 69–73.

27. Quoted in Hutton, *Phil Sheridan*, 63.

28. Quoted in Greene, *Washita*, 129.

29. Quoted in Hatch, *Black Kettle*, 252.

30. Quoted in Hatch, *Black Kettle*, 252.

31. Greene, *Washita*, 136.

32. Hutton, *Phil Sheridan*, 79; Greene, *Washita*, 172.

33. Hardorff, *Washita Memories*, 397.

34. Greene, *Washita*, 135.

35. Hatch, *Black Kettle*, 251.

36. Hatch, *Black Kettle*, 123–28.

37. Quoted in Greene, *Washita*, 162.

38. Quoted in Greene, *Washita*, 165.

39. Quoted in Greene, *Washita*, 166. See also Hoig, *Battle of the Washita*, 190–93.

40. Quoted in Greene, *Washita*, 184.

41. Greene, *Washita*, 173.

42. Quoted in Athearn, *William Tecumseh Sherman*, 274.

43. Greene, *Washita*, 188–92.

CHAPTER 7. MARIAS RIVER

1. Ewers discusses the situation thoroughly in *Blackfeet*, 236–53.

2. Kappler, *Indian Affairs*, 2:552–55.

3. Ewers, *Blackfeet*, 215–21.

4. Graybill, *Red and the White*, 94.

5. Quoted in Ewers, *Blackfeet*, 237.

6. Stout, *Montana*, 339.

7. Hutton, *Phil Sheridan*, 188.

8. Ewers, *Blackfeet*, 241–42.

9. Quoted in Ewers, *Blackfeet*, 244.

10. Ewers, *Blackfeet*, 245.

11. Hutton, *Phil Sheridan*, 188–89.

12. Graybill, *Red and the White*, 98–101; Dunn, *Massacres*, 436–37.

13. Ege, *Tell Baker to Strike Them Hard*, 8–9; Graybill, *Red and the White*, 98–100.

14. Quoted in Ege, *Tell Baker to Strike Them Hard*, 13.

15. Quoted in Graybill, *Red and the White*, 97, 189.

16. Hutton, *Phil Sheridan*, 189.

17. Quoted in Hutton, *Phil Sheridan*, 185.

18. Quoted in Hutton, *Phil Sheridan*, 190.

19. Ege, *Tell Baker to Strike Them Hard*, 29–30; Graybill, *Red and the White*, 107–9.

20. Quoted in Ege, *Tell Baker to Strike Them Hard*, 36–37.

21. Ege, *Tell Baker to Strike Them Hard*, 41–42; Hutton, *Phil Sheridan*, 190–91.

22. Ege, *Tell Baker to Strike Them Hard*, 42–43; Hutton, *Phil Sheridan*, 191.

23. Graybill, *Red and the White*, 126.

24. Schultz, *Blackfeet and Buffalo*, 301. See also Hutton, *Phil Sheridan*, 191; Graybill, *Red and the White*, 125–27; Ege, *Tell Baker to Strike Them Hard*, 43–44.

25. Quoted in Bonney and Bonney, *Battle Drums and Geysers*, 22.

26. Quoted in Graybill, *Red and the White*, 128.

27. Quoted in Graybill, *Red and the White*, 129.

28. Schultz, *Blackfeet and Buffalo*, 300; Dunn, *Massacres*, 440; Hutton, *Phil Sheridan*, 191; Ewers, *Blackfeet*, 250–51; Henderson, "The Piikuni," 62.

29. Quoted in Schultz, *Blackfeet and Buffalo*, 302.

30. Quoted in Ege, *Tell Baker to Strike Them Hard*, 126.

31. Quoted in Graybill, *Red and the White*, 131.

32. Quoted in Graybill, *Red and the White*, 133. See also Ewers, *Blackfeet*, 250–51; Hutton, *Phil Sheridan*, 192.

33. Quoted in Hutton, *Phil Sheridan*, 192, 196.

CHAPTER 8. SKELETON CAVE

1. Browne, *Adventures*, 153. See also Schmitt, *General George Crook*, 163.

2. Goodwin, *Social Organization*, 1; Opler, *Apache Life-Way*, 1–2, 462–64; Lockwood, *Apache Indians*, 1–7.

3. Weber, *Spanish Frontier*, 204–35; Moorhead, *Apache Frontier*, 115–42; Griffen, *Utmost Good Faith*, 190–97; Bourke, *On the Border*, 101–03; Worcester, *Apaches*, 3–9; Goodwin, *Western Apache Raiding*, 12–14.

4. Sweeney, *Cochise*, 142–63; McChristian, *Fort Bowie*, 21–35.

5. Sweeney, *Cochise*, 142–63; McChristian, *Fort Bowie*, 21–35.

6. Jacoby gives the most recent and thorough account in *Shadows at Dawn*. See also Thrapp, *Conquest of Apacheria*, 80–92; Magid, *Gray Fox*, 62–63.

7. Hastings, "Tragedy at Camp Grant," 156.

8. Jacoby, *Shadows at Dawn*, 184–87; Worcester, *Apaches*, 133–34.

9. Quoted in Schmitt, *General George Crook*, 160.

10. Quoted in Magid, *Gray Fox*, 53.

11. Robinson, *General Crook*, 108.

12. Quoted in Schmitt, *General George Crook*, 163–67.

13. Quoted in Magid, *Gray Fox*, 77.

14. Quoted in Thrapp, *Conquest of Apacheria*, 104.

15. Quoted in Thrapp, *Conquest of Apacheria*, 104.

16. Quoted in Bourke, *On the Border*, 151.

17. Ogle, *Federal Control of the Western Apaches*, 100.

18. Thrapp, *Conquest of Apacheria*, 105.

19. Quoted in Schmitt, *General George Crook*, 169.

20. Quoted in Sweeney, *Making Peace with Cochise*, 17 (first quotation), 357 (second quotation), 358–365.

21. Thrapp, *Conquest of Apacheria*, 114.

22. Quoted in Magid, *Gray Fox*, 89.

23. Quoted in Bourke, *On the Border*, 182.

24. Quoted in Thrapp, *Conquest of Apacheria*, 125.

25. Bourke, *On the Border*, 189–92.

26. Quoted in Bourke, *On the Border*, 193.

27. Bourke, *On the Border*, 192–99.

28. Schmitt, *General George Crook*, 177–78; Thrapp, *Conquest of Apacheria*, 135–37.

29. Quoted in Robinson, *General Crook*, 136.

30. Quoted in Schmitt, *General George Crook, 179.*

31. Quoted in Schmitt, *General George Crook*, 179–80.

CHAPTER 9. FORT ROBINSON

1. Greene gives the most recent account of this incident in *January Moon*. See also Hatch, *Black Kettle*, 77–82; Monnett, *"Tell Them,"* 14.

2. Quoted in Hoig, *Perilous Pursuit*, 2.

3. Kappler, *Indian Affairs*, 2:1012–15.

4. Quoted in Hoig, *Perilous Pursuit*, 5.

5. Hyde, *Red Cloud's Folk*, 225.

6. Quoted in Monnett, *"Tell Them,"* 5.

7. Leiker and Powers, *Northern Cheyenne Exodus*, 35–36; Hoig, *Perilous Pursuit*, 21–22.

8. Quoted in Hoig, *Perilous Pursuit*, 22. See also Monnett, *"Tell Them,"* 23–24.

9. Hoig, *Perilous Pursuit*, 22–27; Leiker and Powers, *Northern Cheyenne Exodus*, 37; Monnett, *"Tell Them,"* 37.

10. Quoted in Leiker and Powers, *Northern Cheyenne Exodus*, 37.

11. Hoig, *Perilous Pursuit*, 30–31.

12. Quoted in Leiker and Powers, *Northern Cheyenne Exodus*, 39.

13. Quoted in Hoig, *Perilous Pursuit*, 42 (quotation), 41.

14. Quoted in Grinnell, *Fighting Cheyennes*, 402.

15. Quoted in Hoig, *Perilous Pursuit*, 48.

16. Quoted in Monnett, *"Tell Them,"* 41, 42.

17. Leiker and Powers, *Northern Cheyenne Exodus*, 51–52; Maddux and Maddux, *In Dull Knife's Wake*, 16; Hoig, *Perilous Pursuit*, 54; Monnett, *"Tell Them,"* 43.

18. Hoig, *Perilous Pursuit*, 563–81; Monnett, *"Tell Them,"* 52–56.

19. Leiker and Powers, *Northern Cheyenne Exodus*, 63–65; Hoig, *Perilous Pursuit*, 1376–45; Monnett, *"Tell Them,"* 78–103; Maddux and Maddux, *In Dull Knife's Wake*, 99–132.

20. Monnett, *"Tell Them,"* 110–14; Hoig, *Perilous Pursuit*, 152–54; Greene, *January Moon*, 27–28.

21. Quoted in Monnett, *"Tell Them,"* 115.

22. Monnett, *"Tell Them,"* 115.

23. Quoted in Hoig, *Perilous Pursuit*, 159. See also Greene, *January Moon*, 44–48; Buecker, *Fort Robinson*, 136–37.

24. Grinnell, *Fighting Cheyennes*, 418–19; Leiker and Powers, *Northern Cheyenne Exodus*, 73; Bueker, *Fort Robinson*, 139–40.

25. Quoted in Grinnell, *Fighting Cheyennes*, 420. See also Greene, *January Moon*, 62.

26. Quoted in Hoig, *Perilous Pursuit*, 131–32.

27. Quoted in Monnett, *"Tell Them,"* 132.

28. Leiker and Powers, *Northern Cheyenne Exodus*, 73.

29. Monnett, *"Tell Them,"* 140–41.

30. Monnett, *"Tell Them,"* 151, 153–56; Hoig, *Perilous Pursuit*, 182–92; Greene, *January Moon*, 207. See also Maddux and Maddux, *In Dull Knife's Wake*.

CHAPTER 10. WOUNDED KNEE

1. Ostler, *Plains Sioux*, 66; Greene, *American Carnage*, 19–20.

2. Ostler, *Plains Sioux*, 281–33; Greene, *American Carnage*, 30–33.

3. Greene, *American Carnage*, 38–48; Ostler, *Plains Sioux*, 229–39.

4. Andersson, *Lakota Ghost Dance*, 21.

5. Andrews, "Turning the Tables"; Andersson, *Lakota Ghost Dance*, 22–23.

6. Andersson, *Lakota Ghost Dance*, 27; Utley, *Last Days*, 60–61.

7. Utley, *Last Days*, 61–70; DeMallie, "Lakota Ghost Dance."

8. Quoted in Ostler, *Plains Sioux*, 273.

9. Quoted in Greene, *American Carnage*, 73–74.

10. Quoted in Ostler, *Plains Sioux*, 273–77.

11. Quoted in Utley, *Last Days*, 100.

12. Ostler, *Plains Sioux*, 276–80.

13. Utley, *Last Days*, 111–17.

14. Utley, *Lance and the Shield*, 299–303; Greene, *American Carnage*, 179–82, 186.

15. Quoted in Ostler, *Plains Sioux*, 303.

16. Quoted in Utley, *Last Days*, 181. See also Ostler, *Plains Sioux*, 3278–29; Greene, *American Carnage*, 196–98.

17. Quoted in Ostler, *Plains Sioux*, 330.

18. Quoted in Utley, *Last Days*, 196.

19. Greene, *American Carnage*, 212–14; Ostler, *Plains Sioux*, 335–37; Utley, *Last Days*, 196–99.

20. Quoted in Greene, *American Carnage*, 215.

21. Quoted in Ostler, *Plains Sioux*, 334.

22. Quoted in Utley, *Last Days*, 206.

23. Greene, *American Carnage*, 222–23.

24. Quoted in Andersson, *Whirlwind*, 281.

25. Quoted in Utley, *Last Days*, 208.

26. Quoted in Ostler, *Plains Sioux*, 340.

27. Quoted in Ostler, *Plains Sioux*, 341.

28. Quoted in Andersson, *Whirlwind*, 283.

29. Quoted in Andersson, *Whirlwind*, 229.

30. Quoted in Jensen, Paul, and Carter, *Eyewitness*, 116.

31. Greene, *American Carnage*, 399–400.

32. Quoted in Greene, *American Carnage*, 299, 300–301.

33. Ostler, *Plains Sioux*, 353; Greene, *American Carnage*, 307–9. For discussion of contemporary newspaper coverage of this event, see Jensen, Paul, and Carter, *Eyewitness*, 376–60.

34. Quoted in Porter, *Paper Medicine Man*, 264. See also Greene, *American Carnage*, 308.

35. Quoted in Porter, *Paper Medicine Man*, 264.

Bibliography

U.S. GOVERNMENT PUBLICATIONS

American State Papers: Indian Affairs. 2 vols. Washington, DC: Gales and Seaton, 1832–1861.

Carter, Clarence E., and John Porter Bloom, eds. *The Territorial Papers of the United States.* 27 vols. Washington, DC: GPO, 1934–70.

Commissioner of Indian Affairs. *Annual Reports* (1856 and 1863). Washington, DC: Government Printing Office, 1856, 1863.

Fitzpatrick, John C., ed. *The Writings of George Washington from the Original Manuscript Sources, 1745–1799.* 39 vols. Washington, DC: GPO, 1931–44.

Kappler, Charles J., comp. *Indian Affairs: Laws and Treaties.* 5 vols. Washington, DC: GPO, 1904–41.

U.S. Bureau of the Census. "Indian Wars, Their Cost, and Civil Expenditures." In *Report on Indians Taxed and Indians Not Taxed in the United States (Except Alaska) at the Eleventh Census: 1890,* 637–44. Washington, DC: GPO, 1894.

PUBLISHED PRIMARY SOURCES

Black Hawk. *Black Hawk: An Autobiography.* Ed. Donald Jackson. Urbana: University of Illinois Press, 1964.

Bourke, John Gregory. *On the Border with Crook* (1891). Chicago: Rio Grande Press, 1962.

Browne, J. Ross. *Adventures in Apache Country: A Tour through Arizona and Sonora, 1864*. Ed. Donald M. Powell. Tucson: University of Arizona Press, 1974.

Buecker, Thomas R. *Fort Robinson and the American West, 1874–1899*. Norman: University of Oklahoma Press, 2003.

Coleman, William S. E. *Voices of Wounded Knee*. Lincoln: University of Nebraska Press, 2000.

Commager, Henry Steele, ed. *Documents of American History* (1934). 5th ed. New York: Appleton-Century-Crofts, 1949.

Cooke, Phillip St. George. *Scenes and Adventures of Life in the Army; or the Romance of Military Life* (1857). New York: Arno Press, 1973.

Crockett, David. *The Life of David Crockett* (1834). Facsimile ed. Knoxville: University of Tennessee Press, 1973.

"Declaration of Independence." In *Federal and State Constitutions*, ed. Francis N. Thorpe, 1:3–5. 7 vols. Buffalo, NY: W. S. Hein, 1993.

Doherty, Herbert J. Jr., ed. *Richard Keith Call: Southern Unionist*. Gainesville: University of Florida Press, 1961.

Halbert, Henry S., and T. H. Ball. *The Creek War of 1813 and 1815* (1885). Ed. Frank L. Owsley Jr. Tuscaloosa: University of Alabama Press, 1995.

Hardorff, Richard G., ed. *Washita Memories: Eyewitness Accounts of Custer's Attack on Black Kettle's Village*. Norman: University of Oklahoma Press, 2006.

Hawkins, Benjamin. *Letters, Journals, and Writings of Benjamin Hawkins*. 2 vols. Savannah, GA: Beehive Press, 1980.

Jackson, Andrew. *The Papers of Andrew Jackson*. Ed. Harold D. Moser et al. 10 vols. Knoxville: University of Tennessee Press, 1980–2015.

Jackson, Donald, ed. *Life of Ma-Ka-Tia-Me-She-Kia-Kiak or Black Hawk* (1833). Urbana: University of Illinois Press, 1964.

Jefferson, Thomas. *The Writings of Thomas Jefferson*. Ed. Andrew A. Lipscomb. 20 vols. Washington, DC: Thomas Jefferson Memorial Association, 1905.

Prucha, Francis Paul. *Documents of United States Indian Policy*. 3rd ed. Lincoln: University of Nebraska Press, 2000.

Reynolds, John. *My Own Times: Embracing Also the History of My Life*. Chicago: B. H. Perryman; Belleville, IL: H. L. Davidson, 1855.

Schmitt, Martin F., ed. *General George Crook: His Autobiography*. Norman: University of Oklahoma Press, 1946.

Sheridan, Philip H. *Personal Memoirs of P. H. Sheridan, General, United States Army*. 2 vols. New York: Webster, 1888.

Sweeney, Edwin R., ed. *Making Peace with Cochise: The 1872 Journal of Captain Joseph Alton Sladen*. Norman: University of Oklahoma Press, 1997.

Thorpe, Francis N., ed. *Federal and State Constitutions*. 7 vols. Buffalo, NY: W. W. Hein, 1993.

Whitney, Ellen M., ed. *The Black Hawk War, 1831–1832*. 2 vols. Springfield: Illinois Historical Library, 1970–78.

ARTICLES AND BOOK CHAPTERS

Andrews, Thomas G. "Turning the Tables on Assimilation: Oglala Lakotas and the Pine Ridge Day Schools, 1889–1920s." *Western Historical Quarterly* 33, no. 4 (Winter 2002): 407–30.

Clow, Richmond L. "Mad Bear: William S. Harney and the Sioux Expedition of 1855–1856." *Nebraska History* 61, no. 2 (June 1980): 132–51.

DeMallie, Raymond J., Jr. "The Lakota Ghost Dance: An Ethnohistorical Account." *Pacific Historical Review* 51, no. 4 (November 1982): 385–405.

Ewers, John C. "Intertribal Warfare as the Precursor of Indian-White Warfare on the Northern Great Plains." *Western Historical Quarterly* 6, no. 4 (October 1975): 397–410.

Hastings, James R. "The Tragedy at Camp Grant in 1871." *Arizona and the West* 1, no. 2 (Summer 1959): 146–60.

Henderson, Rodger C. "The Piikuni and the U.S. Army's Piegan Expedition: Competing Narratives of the 1870 Massacre on the Marias River." *Montana The Magazine of Western History* 68, no. 1 (Spring 2018): 48–70.

Holland, James W. "Andrew Jackson and the Creek War." *Alabama Review* 21, no. 4 (1968): 243–75.

Janda, Lance. "Shutting the Gates of Mercy: The American Origins of Total War, 1860–1880." *Journal of Military History* 59, no. 1 (1995): 7–26.

Kanon, Thomas. "A Slow, Laborious Slaughter: The Battle of Horseshoe Bend." *Tennessee Historical Quarterly* 58, no. 1 (Spring 1968): 2–15.

LeCompte, Janet. "Sand Creek," *Colorado Magazine* 41, no. 4 (Fall 1964): 315–35.

Mattison, Ray A., ed. "The Harney Expedition against the Sioux: The Journal of Capt. John B. S. Todd." *Nebraska History* 45, no. 2 (June 1962): 89–130.

McCann, Lloyd E. "The Grattan Massacre." *Nebraska History* 37, no. 1 (April 1956): 1–26.

Mellon, William J. "The Military Investigation of Chivington." *Chronicles of Oklahoma* 16, no. 4 (1938): 444–64.

Ostler, Jeffrey. "Genocide and American Indian History." *Oxford Research Encyclopedia of American History* (March 2015), https://oxfordre.com/americanhistory/view/10.1093/acrefore/9780199329175.001.0001/acrefore-9780199329175-e-3, accessed June 16, 2020.

Price, Catherine. "Lakotas and Euroamericans: Contrasted Concepts of 'Chieftainship' and Decision-Making Authority." *Ethnohistory* 41, no. 3 (Summer 1994): 447–63.

Wallace, Anthony F. C. "Prelude to Disaster: The Course of Indian-White Relations Which Led to the Black Hawk War of 1832." In *The Black Hawk War, 1831–1832*, ed. Ellen M. Whitney. 1:1–51. 2 vols. Springfield: Illinois Historical Library, 1970–78.

Wolfe, Patrick. "Settler Colonialism and the Elimination of the Native." *Journal of Genocide Research* 8 (December 2006): 387–409.

BOOKS

Adams, G. Rollie. *General William S. Harney: Prince of Dragoons*. Lincoln: University of Nebraska Press, 2001.

Anderson, Gary Clayton. *Ethnic Cleansing and the Indian: The Crime That Should Haunt America*. Norman: University of Oklahoma Press, 2014.

Andersson, Rani-Henrik. *The Lakota Ghost Dance of 1890*. Lincoln: University of Nebraska Press, 2008.

———. *A Whirlwind Passed through Our Country: Lakota Voices of the Ghost Dance*. Norman: University of Oklahoma Press, 2018.

Athearn, Robert G. *William Tecumseh Sherman and the Settlement of the West*. Norman: University of Oklahoma Press, 1956.

Barnes, Henry Elmer. *Perpetual War for Perpetual Peace: A Critical Examination of the Foreign Policy of Franklin Delano Roosevelt and Its Aftermath*. Caldwell, ID: Caxton Printers, 1953.

Beck, Paul N. *The First Sioux War: The Grattan Fight and Blue Water Creek, 1854–1856*. New York: University Press of America, 2004.

Berkhofer, Robert F. *The White Man's Indian: Images of the American Indian from Columbus to the Present*. New York: Knopf, 1978.

Berthrong, Donald J. *The Southern Cheyennes*. Norman: University of Oklahoma Press, 1963.

Bonney, Orrin H., and Lorraine Bonney. *Battle Drums and Geysers: The Life and Journals of Lt. Gustavus Cheyney Doane, Soldier and Explorer of the Yellowstone and Snake River Regions*. Chicago: Sage Books, 1970.

Borneman, Walter R. *1812: The War That Forged a Nation*. New York: HarperCollins, 2004.

Brown, Dee. *Bury My Heart at Wounded Knee: An Indian History of the American West*. New York: Holt, Rinehart and Winston, 1970.

Buecker, Thomas R. *Fort Robinson and the American West, 1874-1899*. Norman: University of Oklahoma Press, 2003.

Caughey, John W. *McGillivray of the Creeks*. Norman: University of Oklahoma Press, 1938.

Chalfant, William Y. *Cheyennes and Horse Soldiers: The 1857 Expedition and the Battle of Solomon's Fork*. Norman: University of Oklahoma Press, 1989.

Christensen, Scott R. *Sagwitch: Shoshone Chieftain, Mormon Elder, 1822–1887*. Logan: Utah State University Press, 1999.

Clifton, James A. *Being and Becoming Indian: Biographical Studies of North American Frontiers*. Chicago: Dorsey Press, 1989.

Coffman, Edward M. *The Old Army: A Portrait of the American Army in Peacetime, 1784–1898*. New York: Oxford University Press, 1986.

Cole, Cyrenus. *I Am a Man: The Indian Black Hawk*. Iowa City: State Historical Society of Iowa, 1938.

Coward, John M. *The Newspaper Indian: Native American Identity in the Press, 1820–90*. Urbana: University of Illinois Press, 1999.

Dippie, Brian. *The Vanishing American: White Attitudes and United States Indian Policy*. Lawrence: University Press of Kansas, 1991.

Divine, Robert. *Perpetual War for Perpetual Peace*. College Station: Texas A&M University Press, 2004.

Donovan, James. *A Terrible Glory: Custer and the Little Big Horn—The Last Great Battle of the American West*. New York: Little, Brown, 2008.

Dowd, Gregory Evans. *A Spirited Resistance: The North American Indian Struggle for Unity, 1745–1815*. Baltimore: Johns Hopkins University Press, 1992.

Dunn, J. P. *Massacres of the Mountains: A History of the Indian Wars of the Far West* (1886). New York: Capricorn Books, 1969.

Ege, Robert J. *Tell Baker to Strike Them Hard: Incident on the Marias, 23 Jan. 1870*. Bellview, NE: Old Army Press, 1970.

Ethridge, Robbie F. *Creek Country: The Creek Indians and Their World*. Chapel Hill: University of North Carolina Press, 2003.

Ewers, John C. *The Blackfeet: Raiders on the Northwestern Plains*. Norman: University of Oklahoma Press, 1976.

Fleisher, Kass. *The Bear River Massacre and the Making of History*. Albany: State University of New York Press, 2004.

Foley, William E. *Wilderness Journey: The Life of William Clark*. Columbia: University of Missouri Press, 2004.

Fowler, Loretta, American Council of Learned Societies, and Fred Eggan. *Arapahoe Politics, 1851–1978: Symbol of Crises in Authority*. Lincoln: University of Nebraska Press, 1986.

Frank, Andrew. *Creeks and Southerners: Biculturalism on the Early American Frontier*. Lincoln: University of Nebraska Press, 2005.

Goodwin, Grenville. *The Social Organization of the Western Apache*. Tucson: University of Arizona Press, 2016.

———. *Western Apache Raiding and Warfare*. Ed. Keith H. Basso. Tucson: University of Arizona Press, 1973.

Greene, Jerome. *January Moon: The Northern Cheyenne Breakout from Fort Robinson, 1878–1879*. Norman: University of Oklahoma Press, 2020.

———. *Washita: The U.S. Army and the Southern Cheyennes*. Norman: University of Oklahoma Press, 2004.

Grandin, Greg. *The End of the Myth: From the Frontier to the Border Wall in the Mind of America*. New York: Macmillan, 2019.

Graybill, Andrew R. *The Red and the White: A Family Saga of The American West*. New York: Liveright, 2013.

Green, Michael D. "McGillivray, Alexander." In *Encyclopedia of North American Indians*. New York: Houghton Mifflin, 1996.

———. *The Politics of Indian Removal: Creek Government and Society in Crisis*. Lincoln: University of Nebraska Press, 1982.

Greene, Jerome. *American Carnage: Wounded Knee, 1890*. Norman: University of Oklahoma Press, 2014.

——. *January Moon: The Northern Cheyenne Breakout from Fort Robinson, 1878–1879*. Norman: University of Oklahoma Press, 2020.

——. *Washita: The U.S. Army and the Southern Cheyennes, 1867–1869*. Norman: University of Oklahoma Press, 2004.

Griffen, William B. *Utmost Good Faith: Patterns of Apache-Mexican Hostilities in Northern Chihuahua Border Warfare, 1821–1848*. Albuquerque: University of New Mexico Press, 1989.

Griffith, Benjamin W., Jr. *McIntosh and Weatherford, Creek Indian Leaders*. Tuscaloosa: University of Alabama Press, 1988.

Grinnell, George Bird. *The Fighting Cheyennes*. Norman: University of Oklahoma Press, 1956.

Hagan, William T. *The Sac and Fox Indians*. Norman: University of Oklahoma Press, 1958.

Hall, John W. *Uncommon Defense: Indian Allies in the Black Hawk War*. Cambridge, MA: Harvard University Press, 2009.

Hatch, Thom. *Black Kettle: The Cheyenne Chief Who Sought Peace But Found War*. Hoboken, NJ: John Wiley, 2004.

Henri, Florette. *The Southern Indians and Benjamin Hawkins, 1796–1816*. Norman: University of Oklahoma Press, 1986.

Hoig, Stan. *The Battle of the Washita: the Sheridan-Custer Campaign of 1867–68*. Garden City, NY: Doubleday, 1976.

——. *The Peace Chiefs of the Cheyennes*. Norman: University of Oklahoma Press, 1980.

——. *Perilous Pursuit: The U.S. Cavalry and the Northern Cheyennes*. Boulder: University Press of Colorado, 2000.

——. *The Sand Creek Massacre*. Norman: University of Oklahoma Press, 1961.

Hutton, Paul Andrew. *Phil Sheridan and His Army*. Lincoln: University of Nebraska Press, 1985.

Hyde, George E. *Life of George Bent, Written from His Letters*. Edited by Savoie Lottinville. Norman: University of Oklahoma Press, 1968.

——. *Red Cloud's Folk: A History of the Oglala Sioux* (1937). Norman: University of Oklahoma Press, 1967.

Jacoby, Karl J. *Shadows at Dawn: An Apache Massacre and the Violence of History*. New York: Penguin Books, 2008.

Jensen, Richard E., R. Eli Paul, and John E. Carter. *Eyewitness at Wounded Knee*. Lincoln: Universty of Nebraska Press, 2011.

Jones, Douglas C. *The Treaty of Medicine Lodge: The Story of the Great Treaty Council as Told by Eyewitnesses*. Norman: University of Oklahoma Press, 1966.

Jung, Patrick P. *The Black Hawk War of 1832*. Norman: University of Oklahoma Press, 2007.

Kanon, Thomas. *Tennesseans at War, 1812–1815: Andrew Jackson, the Creek War, and the Battle of New Orleans*. Tuscaloosa: University of Alabama Press, 2014.

Kelman, Ari. *A Misplaced Massacre: Struggling over the Memory of Sand Creek*. Cambridge, MA: Harvard University Press, 2015.

Kraft, Louis. *Sand Creek and the Tragic End of a Lifeway*. Norman: University of Oklahoma Press, 2020.

Kvasnicka, Robert M., and Herman J. Viola, eds. *The Commissioners of Indian Affairs, 1824–1971*. Lincoln: University of Nebraska Press, 1979.

Leiker, James N., and Ramon Powers. *The Northern Cheyenne Exodus in History and Memory*. Norman: University of Oklahoma Press, 2011.

Lepore, Jill. *The Name of War: King Philip's War and the Origins of American Identity*. New York: Alfred A. Knopf, 1998.

Lockwood, Frank C. *The Apache Indians*. Lincoln: University of Nebraska Press, 1987.

Maddux, Vernon R., and Albert Maddux. *In Dull Knife's Wake: The True Story of the Northern Cheyenne Exodus of 1878*. Norman, OK: Horse Creek Publishers, 2003.

Madley, Benjamin. *An American Genocide: The United States and the California Indian Catastrophe*. New Haven: Yale University Press, 2016.

Madsen, Brigham D. *Glory Hunter: A Biography of Patrick Edward Connor*. Salt Lake City: University of Utah Press, 1990.

———. *The Shoshoni Frontier and the Bear River Massacre*. Salt Lake City: University of Utah Press, 1985.

Magid, Paul. *The Gray Fox: George Crook and the Indian Wars*. Norman: University of Oklahoma Press, 2015.

Martin, Joel W. *Sacred Revolt: The Muskogees' Struggle for a New World*. Boston: Beacon Press, 1991.

McCarthy, Cormac. *Blood Meridian or the Evening Redness in the West*. New York: Random House, 1985.

McChristian, Douglas. *Fort Bowie, Arizona: Combat Post of the Southwest, 1858–1894*. Norman: University of Oklahoma Press, 2005.

McDermott, John D., R. Eli Paul, and Sandra J. Lowry, eds. *All Because of a Mormon Cow: Historical Accounts of the Grattan Massacre, 1854–1855*. Norman: University of Oklahoma Press, 2018.

McMurtry, Larry. *Oh What a Slaughter: Massacres in the American West, 1846–1890*. New York: Simon and Schuster, 2005.

Michno, Gregory F. *Battle at Sand Creek: The Military Perspective*. El Segundo, CA: Upton and Sons, 2004.

———. *Encyclopedia of Indian Wars: Western Battles and Skirmishes 1850–1890*. Missoula, MT: Mountain Press, 2003.

Miller, Rod. *Massacre at Bear River*. Caldwell, ID: Caxton Press, 2008.

Monnett, John H. *The Battle of Beecher Island and the Indian War of 1867–68*. Boulder: University Press of Colorado, 1992.

———. *"Tell Them We Are Going Home": The Odyssey of the Northern Cheyennes*. Norman: University of Oklahoma Press, 2001.

Moorhead, Max L. *The Apache Frontier: Jacob Ugarte and Spanish-Indian Relations in Northern New Spain, 1769–1791*. Civilization of the American Indian Series 90. Norman: University of Oklahoma Press, 1968.

Nichols, David A. *Lincoln and the Indians: Civil War Policy and Politics*. Columbia: University of Missouri Press, 1978.

Nichols, Roger L. *American Indians in U.S. History* (2003). 2nd ed. Norman: University of Oklahoma Press, 2014.

———. *Black Hawk and the Warrior's Path* (1992). 2nd ed. New York: Wiley Blackwell, 2017.

———. *General Henry Atkinson: A Western Military Career*. Norman: University of Oklahoma Press, 1965.

Ogle, Ralph, Hedrick. *Federal Control of the Western Apaches*. Albuquerque: University of New Mexico Press, 1940.

Opler, Morris E. *An Apache Life-Way: The Economic, Social, and Religious Institutions of the Chiricahua Indians* (1941). Lincoln: University of Nebraska, 1996.

Osborn, William M. *The Wild Frontier: Atrocities during the American-Indian Wars from Jamestown Colony to Wounded Knee*. New York: Random House, 2000.

Ostler, Jeffrey. *The Plains Sioux and U.S. Colonialism from Lewis and Clark to Wounded Knee*. New York: Cambridge University Press, 2004.

Owsley, Frank L. *The Struggle for the Gulf Borderlands: The Creek War and the Battle of New Orleans, 1812–1815*. Gainesville: University Presses of Florida, 1981.

Paul, R. Eli. *Blue Water Creek and the First Sioux War*. Norman: University of Oklahoma Press, 2004.

———. *The Frontier Army: Episodes from Dakota and the West*. Pierre: South Dakota Historical Society, 2019.

Porter, Joseph C. *Paper Medicine Man: John Gregory Bourke and His American West*. Norman: University of Oklahoma Press, 1986.

Powell, Peter J. *People of the Sacred Mountain: A History of the Northern Cheyenne Chiefs and Warrior Societies, 1830–1879*. 2 vols. San Francisco: Harper and Row, 1981.

Power, Samantha. *"A Problem from Hell": America and the Age of Genocide*. New York: Basic Books, 2002.

Prucha, Francis Paul. *American Indian Treaties: The History of a Political Anomaly*. Berkeley: University of California Press, 1994.

———. *The Great Father: The United States Government and the Indians*. 2 vols. Lincoln: University of Nebraska Press, 1984.

———. *Guide to the Military Posts of the United States*. Madison: State Historical Society of Wisconsin, 1964.

———. *The Sword of the Republic: The United States Army on the Frontier, 1783–1864*. New York: Macmillan, 1969.

Remini, Robert. *Andrew Jackson and His Indian Wars*. New York: Viking, 2001.

Reston, James. *Sherman's March and Vietnam*. New York: Macmillan, 1984.

Robinson, Charles M., III. *General Crook and the Western Frontier*. Norman: University of Oklahoma Press, 2001.

———. *A Good Year to Die: The Story of the Great Sioux War*. New York: Random House, 1995.

Rockwell, Stephen J. *Indian Affairs and the Administrative State in the Nineteenth Century.* New York: Cambridge University Press, 2010.

Saunt, Claudio. *A New Order of Things: Property, Power, and the Transformation of the Creek Indians, 1733–1816.* New York: Cambridge University Press, 1999.

Schultz, James Willard. *Blackfeet and Buffalo: Memories of a Life among the Blackfeet.* Norman: University of Oklahoma Press, 1962.

Shannon, Donald H. *The Boise Massacre on the Oregon Trail: Attack on the Ward Party in 1854 and Massacres of 1859.* Caldwell, ID: Snake Country Publishing, 2004.

———. *The Utter Disaster on the Oregon Trail: The Utter and Van Ornum Massacres of 1860.* Caldwell, ID: Snake Country Publishing, 1993.

Stannard, David. *American Holocaust: The Conquest of the New World.* New York: Oxford University Press, 1992.

Stout, Tom. *Montana, Its Story and Biography: A History of Aboriginal and Territorial Montana and Three Decades of Statehood.* Chicago: American Historical Society, 1921.

Sugden, John. *Tecumseh: A Life.* New York: Henry Holt, 1997.

Sully, Langdon. *No Tears for the General: The Life of Alfred Sully, 1821–1879.* Palo Alto, CA: American West, 1974.

Svaldi, David. *Sand Creek and the Rhetoric of Extermination: A Case Study in Indian-White Relations.* Lanham, MD: University Press of America, 1989.

Sweeney, Edwin R. *Cochise, Chiricahua Apache Chief.* Norman: University of Oklahoma Press, 1991.

Takaki, Ronald. *A Different Mirror.* New York: Little, Brown, 1993.

Thornton, Russell. *American Indian Holocaust and Survival: A Population History since 1492.* Norman: University of Oklahoma Press, 1987.

Thrapp, Dan L. *The Conquest of Apacheria.* Norman: University of Oklahoma Press, 1967.

Trask, Kerry A. *Black Hawk: The Battle for the Heart of America.* New York: Henry Holt, 2006.

Unruh, John D. Jr. *The Plains Across: The Overland Emigrants and the Trans-Mississippi West, 1840–60.* Urbana: University of Illinois Press, 1979.

Utley, Robert M. *Frontier Regulars: The United States Army and the Indian, 1866–1891.* New York: Macmillan, 1973.

———. *Frontiersmen in Blue: The United States Army and the Indian, 1848–1865.* New York: Macmillan, 1967.

———. *The Indian Frontier of the American West, 1846–1890.* Albuquerque: University of New Mexico Press, 1984.

———. *The Lance and the Shield: The Life and Times of Sitting Bull.* New York: Henry Holt, 1993.

———. *The Last Days of the Sioux Nation.* New Haven: Yale University Press, 1963.

Varley, James F. *Brigham and the Brigadier: General Patrick Connor and His California Volunteers in Utah and along the Overland Trail.* Tucson, AZ: Westernlore Press, 1989.

Vidal, Gore. *Perpetual War for Perpetual Peace: How We Got to Be So Hated*. New York: Thunder's Mouth Press, 2002.

Viola, Herman J. *Diplomats in Buckskin: A History of Indian Delegations in Washington City*. Washington, DC: Smithsonian Press, 1981.

Waselkov, Gregory A. *A Conquering Spirit: Fort Mims and the Red Stick War of 1813–1814*. Tuscaloosa: University of Alabama Press, 2006.

Weber, David J. *The Spanish Frontier in North America*. New Haven: Yale University Press, 1992.

Weigley, Russell F. *The American Way of War: A History of United States Military Strategy and Policy*. New York: Macmillan, 1973.

West, Elliott. *The Contested Plains: Indians, Gold Seekers, and the Rush to Colorado*. Lawrence: University Press of Kansas, 1998.

Wilhelm, Thomas. *A Military Dictionary and Gazetteer*. Rev. ed. Philadelphia: L. R. Hamersley, 1881.

Worcester, Donald E. *The Apaches: Eagles of the Southwest*. Norman: University of Oklahoma Press, 1979.

Wright, J. Leitch. *Creeks and Seminoles: The Destruction and Regeneration of the Muscogulge People*. Lincoln: University of Nebraska Press, 1986.

Wylie, Paul R. *Blood on the Marias: The Baker Massacre*. Norman: University of Oklahoma Press, 2016.

Index